THE NEW
WEALTH
PARADIGM

FOR FINANCIAL FREEDOM

DR. ALBERT (ACE) GOERIG

The New Wealth Paradigm

by Dr. Albert "Ace" Goerig

ISBNs: 978-0-9753339-4-5 (softcover print)
978-0-9753339-5-2 (eBook)

Published by

Doctor Ace LLC

222 Lilly Rd. NE
Olympia, WA 98506
DoctorAce.com

Contents

DISCLAIMER

This guide is for informational and educational purposes only, based on the personal experience and research of the author. Information has been obtained from data sources considered to be reliable, but its accuracy and completeness are not guaranteed. This guide is offered with the understanding that the author and publisher are neither fiduciaries nor engaged in rendering legal, tax, investment, financial, or other advice. All content is general in nature, and your unique circumstances may include factors not considered by the author.

You assume sole responsibility for evaluating the merits and risks of the provided content, as well as that of any third-party websites, providers, or resources mentioned by the author. It is recommended that you conduct appropriate due diligence and consult with professional advisers. The author and publisher specifically disclaim any liability or loss arising from your use, application, or interpretation, directly or indirectly, of any information herein or any referenced third-party resource.

Preface

FREEDOM IS WHEN YOU HAVE the lifestyle options and personal wealth to enjoy life on your own terms now and in the future. It means working the days you want, providing for your family at a very high level, building true wealth with lifelong financial security, and never experiencing a day of financial stress again in your life.

Achieving that level of success largely depends on informed personal business choices and understanding our financial systems for growing your wealth and managing it effectively. Over the past few years, the banks, along with other financial institutions and advisers, have created a false narrative of financial advice and investing, making it near impossible for most Americans to retire with dignity. This guide will help you understand the flaws associated with 401(k)s, IRAs, and investing in the stock-market casino. Instead I will show you a simple, safe, and stress-free approach to maximize today's financial landscape which will dramatically accelerate your path to financial and personal freedom.

To your success and happiness,

[signature]

Introduction

"Two roads diverged in a wood, and I—I took the one less traveled by, and that has made all the difference."

— Robert Frost

Historical Context

HOW DID WE GET INTO SUCH A MESS?

THE SILENT GENERATION was born between 1925 and 1945 during the Great Depression and World War II. They had stable jobs with some type of pension or defined benefit plan that guaranteed them a specific (defined) amount of money for each month of retirement, adjusted to inflation for life.

This generation paid off debt early, paid cash for purchases, and had no credit cards. They did not gamble in the stock market and had whole-life insurance policies which could be harvested for cash value in case of emergencies, investments, or other financial necessities.

It's estimated that more than 50% of savings went into cash-value whole-life insurance. It was safe, protected, and provided a predictable future income for decades while reducing dependence on banks. This approach to finances allowed the Silent Generation to create incredible and stable wealth. The death benefit from their whole-life insurance policy provided an income tax-free legacy for their spouse and children, known as the Baby Boomers. This was a financial model that worked.

In the 1970s and 1980s, the Baby Boomers (born between 1946 and 1964) were introduced to term life insurance, credit cards, long-term mortgages, 401(k)s, and investing in the stock market. From 1982 up to the year 2000, there was a long-term bull market, in which the S&P 500 averaged annually around 14% and 18% with dividends. But even though the S&P 500 did very well, the average investor made less than 5%.

Financial institutions touted the stock market as the best and only way to save for your retirement and to get rich. These institutions created a smoke-and-mirror system that would secretly take up to 80% of the individual's return and keep it for themselves. Even today, most investors do not understand this scam and will never reach financial independence. The Baby Boomers had forgotten or not learned the simple lessons from their parents: Getting out of debt early and paying cash for purchases was the fastest, safest, and most predictable way to become financially independent.

Long-term bull markets are followed by long-term bear markets, which occurred at the beginning of the year 2000. At that point, the S&P 500 was at 1500. Today, 20 years later, it is around 3200—an increase of a little over 119% in 20 years. That is a taxed annualized return of 4.1%, and, with dividends reinvested, it would be 6%. Adjusted for inflation, the average return would be 3.8% before tax. That is remarkably close to the 3.88% annual gain investors in equity mutual funds have earned over the past two decades, according to the independent research firm DALBAR.

Also, in 2000, the S&P 500 reached an all-time high, which was immediately followed by a two-year negative 49% drop. Similarly, the NASDAQ technology index plunged 78% between

March 10, 2000 and October 9, 2002. After that, in 2007, there was another S&P all-time high followed by a negative 56% drop in value over the next two years.

Since 2009, we have been in a long-term bull market that is again reaching all-time highs, but in March 2020, the market dropped 34% and rebounded back over the next few months to all-time highs. No one knows what will happen next in the stock market or to your personal portfolio and 401(k). Many investors fear a significant correction, especially after the 2020 US national election.

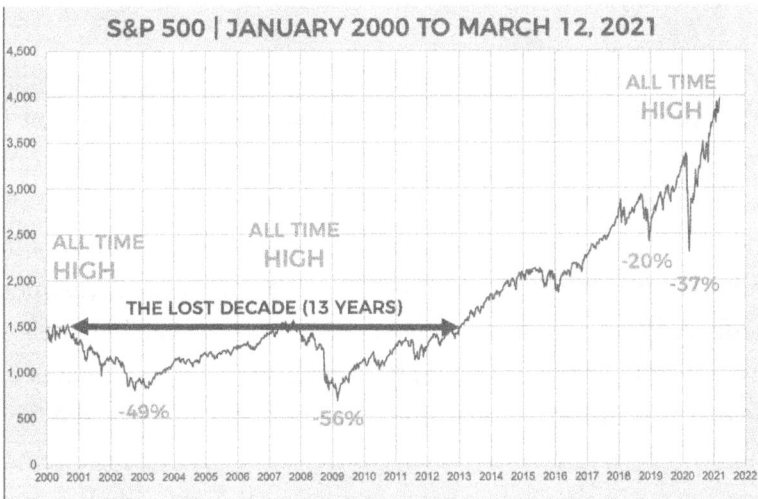

S&P 500 | JANUARY 2000 TO MARCH 12, 2021

According to the *Wall Street Journal,* Americans approaching retirement age will have to trade their golden years for a retirement filled with scrimping and sacrifice:

"Their median incomes, including Social Security and retirement-fund payments haven't risen in years, they have high debt, are often paying off children's educations, and are dipping into savings for aging parents. The average 401(k) retirement funds will bring in a median income of under $8,000 a year for a household of two."

Furthermore, Social Security is predicted to be just a few years away from paying out more than it takes in. The fund will "become depleted." Sources differ, but the story remains the same.

According to a 2018 study by Northwestern Mutual, 21% of Americans have no retirement savings, and an additional 10% have less than $5,000 in savings. A third of Baby Boomers currently in, or approaching, retirement age has between nothing and $25,000 set aside. There is no doubt that this model has failed.

THE BIG LIES

Over the past 50 years, Americans have been taught by banks, the government, financial advisers, and financial institutions to stay in debt while also telling them that the only way to become wealthy and retire comfortably is to accept risk, volatility, and unpredictability in the stock-market casino through 401(k) plans and other financial vehicles that they control. These investment models will take away two-thirds of your disposable income and freedom while keeping you broke, unable to retire, and in debt for the rest of your life. You become their cash cow until you die. This book will help you learn a simple, safe, and predictable system to create wealth, obtain your personal and financial freedom, and leave a legacy for your family.

The late John Bogle, the father of the indexed mutual fund, warned us against the hefty fees of active managers and the effect on our potential return. For a typical investor, a 2.5% fee will take 80% of their compounding returns and put it into the hands of the fund manager and financial adviser, not the investor. Fees of only 1% per year can slash the value of your savings by 28% over the next 35 years, according to the Department of Labor. These are in addition to other fees in actively managed funds such as trading costs, taxes, and hidden fees.

"You must unlearn what you have learned."

— Yoda

As Yoda taught in *Star Wars,* the first step is letting go of how you have been programmed in the past. This guide shows you a simple, safe, stress-free, and predictable approach to quickly become debt-free and financially free on your own.

Let me show you the road less traveled so you can take charge and control of your own money—and stop playing the bankers, advisers, and financial-institutions game. The new model described in this book will eliminate your money stress and bring peace back into your life.

ACHIEVING FINANCIAL FREEDOM

Creating wealth is not complicated! There is no need to take risks in the stock market while we have investment and saving vehicles that are safe, predictable, and guaranteed as described later in this guide.

The secret to becoming financially free is to know how to invest your money without risk while receiving a guaranteed tax-free return. These options are never offered to you because no one makes money off them. What you are offered are risky stocks and mutual funds with high commissions and advisory fees, along with the high anxiety associated with these products.

Most of your advisers will not appreciate these paradigm-shift concepts because each of them looks through a different lens based on their experience, training, and what they will make from you. Each has a different agenda for you and your money. You need to create your own agenda that works best for you.

Your banker's motivation is to get your money into their bank, pay you no interest, and then loan your money to you at an extremely high interest rate.

Your CPA gets paid to do your state and federal income-tax returns, save you taxes, and keep you out of tax difficulty. Because most accountants do not understand business and are risk-averse, their advice would be not to invest in business growth through business-management coaching because they cannot understand the benefits, and they see it as just an expense. Surprisingly, some CPAs are concerned that an increase in your net income would increase your taxes, and that would be a bad thing. CPAs also recommend that you put your money in 401(k)s to save taxes—which is possibly the worst place to invest your money.

Your investment adviser will encourage you to put your money into their recommended investments and a 401(k) plan, so they can continue to receive fees that take most of your investment returns, even when you lose money in the market. When it comes to your money, you are the only one who cares more about it than any of your advisers.

Everyone needs to focus on what investment of their time and money produces the greatest and safest returns. If you correctly execute the strategies outlined in this guide, then you will have more money than you will ever need and provide a secure financial future for you and your family. That is true wealth that you can trade for time, freedom, and choices.

You will learn how to be completely debt-free in 7 to 10 years. I will show you the best strategies to safely get the best returns for yourself, without paying the extraordinarily high fees and commissions of financial advisers and brokers. You must understand that investing in the stock market is gambling, and you should not put more than 5 to 10% of your excess money in that modality. Once you understand the concept in this book, you will never need to invest in the stock-market casino.

Financial Myths and Mistakes That Keep Us Poor

OVER THE PAST 60 YEARS, we have been imprinted through our culture with financial myths, half-truths, and lies by those who want to take our discretionary income and keep us poor. Once we look closely at the myths, we realize how these lies keep us from reaching true personal and financial freedom.

Myth 1: Pay yourself first, and save and invest.

When you put your money in your bank savings account, you only get a taxable .1% return. The average investor has made less than 4% annually of taxable return over the past 20 years. The best investment for your disposable income is to pay off debt, which will give you immediately more than **double your return** on your investment and is the fastest way to become wealthy. I will show you how in the next chapters.

Myth 2: Why pay off a 3.5% interest rate home loan when I can make 7% investing?

There are many advisers who wrongly tell you to keep your 30-year mortgage and put your excess money into their so-called investments instead of paying it off early. They talk about lost-opportunity costs. What these people don't want you to understand is that the **true average home loan interest rate over the 30 years is 50% but is more than 100% for the first 15 years of your mortgage.** The only time the interest rate is 3.5% is the last year of your mortgage. By paying off debt early, you can get a tax-free guaranteed 100% return on your money without risk. Most people will lose their discretionary income in investments because they do not know how to invest safely and will possibly lose most of their money in their adviser's fees and investment misadventures.

One of the biggest misconceptions that banks and accountants perpetuate is that you should not pay off your house early because you can write off the interest on your taxes. If we look at this closely, in 2020, an average American couple who paid $10,000 a year in interest had the choice of either taking the standard deduction of $24,000 or to itemize their return and take the $10,000 tax write-off. When they itemize, they are unable to take the standard deduction of $24,000 and have an overall loss of $14,000.

The two best investments you can make is to pay off all your debts early while at the same time investing in yourself through some type of business-management coaching to learn how to make more money.

Myth 3: Maximize your IRA and 401k plan early and yearly.

Retirement plans and their investments benefit only the financial advisers, brokers, mutual-fund companies, and the IRS. Here are the problems with tax-deferred investing. In Michael Reese's book, *The Big Retirement Lie,* he gives an example of you being 30 years old and putting $6,000 a year in an IRA, saving $1,800 per year in taxes. Over the next 35 years, you will have contributed $210,000 to the plan and saved $63,000 in taxes. If the plan grows at 8%, at age 65, you will have a balance of $1,075,257. When you turn 65, you will have to pay back to the government a total of $460,000 over the next 20 years. And when you die, your children can pay back another $300,000 to the government on top of what you have already paid. In summary, the government loans you $63,000, and you and your children pay the IRS back $760,000. Does that sound like a good deal to you?

Wall Street has hijacked these retirement plans. The excessive fees charged by mutual-fund companies and plan administrators are robbing you of up to half of your nest egg. The government can change the rules to these 401(k)s and IRAs at any time, as they did with the Roth IRA, and drastically reduce any true benefit of these plans. A majority of these plans are defined-contribution plans, which define how much you can put in each year, but you have no idea what will be available when you retire and start taking money out. Nor do you know how much taxes you will be paying on that money, which could be as much as 50%. This is completely different from a pension plan or defined-benefit plan that gives you a specific benefit or amount that you can rely upon when you withdraw your money. Here are some of the other problems associated with these plans.

Taxes are deferred, not eliminated, and you will still have to pay the tax on the money in retirement when you need the money most. The tax rate could be higher, even up to 70% when you retire, like they were in the past. You just do not know. You can lose 50% to 80% of your retirement plan return through the 2% to 3% fees from financial advisers using actively managed mutual funds. Your money is locked up like in a prison, and you cannot access it until age 59½ without penalty. You must take out minimum distributions at 70½ or pay a large penalty. The market has averaged a before-tax return of only 3.88%

over the last 20 years. You cannot write off any losses. As an owner, you must pay all fees and expenses of the plan plus pay for your employees.

There is no difference in tax savings whether the taxes are taken away from you at the beginning or at the end (tax-deferred). It's the same fraction of your money that is left to you. Most people look at their retirement savings and think it's all theirs but have forgotten that Uncle Sam will share in every penny you've put in and every penny of growth. You would be better off investing on your own and paying the smaller 20% capital gains taxes, instead of paying 35% to 70% in ordinary income tax.

Myth 4: Financial-adviser myth.

There is an old saying, "A broker is someone who will invest your money until you are broke." You must understand that advisers, brokers, and mutual-fund managers are salespeople. They charge 1 to 4% of your entire portfolio even when you lose money. They will take 50% to 80% of your gains.

If you invest $4,000 per month for 30 years at 7% return you will earn $3,781,475. What will your financial advisors and mutual fund take from your earnings when they charge only 1%, 2%, 3% or 4% fees?

Advisor/Fund % Fee	Advisor/Fund will take from you	% Return of Your Earnings
1%	$962,332	25%
2%	$1,725,989	46%
3%	$2,332,230	62%
4%	$2,820,600	75%

As you can see in the chart above, they will take from you up to 75% of your earnings. They will even get their fees even when you lose money that year. You need to learn how to invest your money safely without financial advisors.

Many will continuously buy and sell stocks resulting in transaction fees and taxes. Most of these financial "experts" make you think that investing is complex and difficult in order to confuse you to invest through them. They will use terms such as "modern portfolio design" or "asset allocations" to confuse you, so you don't learn how simple it is to invest on your own.

You will do better than 96% of most advisers by investing on your own into the S&P 500 or the US total stock market index funds through companies like Charles Schwab and Vanguard. Remember, investing in the stock market is gambling and is known as the "Wall Street Casino" where return on investment is never guaranteed. Later in this book, you will find out how to get a guaranteed tax-free return of 4% to 5% without the stock market.

Myth 5: We need banks to obtain personal and business loans.

In this book, you will learn how to create your own Personal Bank and borrow from yourself. This will allow you to save thousands of dollars when you need to borrow money. When the bank lends you $100,000, all they need is $10,000 in the bank, making them a more-than 100% return. If you need to borrow money during hard times, they probably will not give you a loan. You do not get any interest on the money in your checking account, and you might earn 0.2% in your bank savings account, which will be taxed. Their number-one-tier asset is whole-life insurance policies on their executives. Using this same mechanism, you can create your own Personal Bank through high-cash-value, whole-life insurance and borrow from yourself and not your bank.

Myth 6: Buy only term life insurance, and invest the difference.

The problem with this concept is that people don't invest the difference. They most likely rent the term, lapse it, and spend the difference. Less than 1% of all term policies ever pay a death benefit. You would be better off using the money from your term policy premiums to buy a high-cash-value, whole-life insurance policy. Most insurance salesmen are unaware of this type of policy, so for more information, go to PersonalBank4U.com.

Myth 7: Emergency-fund myth.

Some financial advisers recommend saving three to six months of living expenses in an emergency fund before you start paying off debt. The problem with this approach is that you never get around to paying off the debt, because it takes about two years to save up that amount. Meanwhile, many people take out the money for non-emergency items.

You must begin to see debt as a tax, and automatically pay 10% to 20% of your monthly income toward the principal on your debt. Once your credit cards are paid off, you do have an emergency fund. You can get a line of credit or home-equity loan, or you can just stop paying those accelerated payments for one or two months. If you feel you need some money set aside, put $1,000 into a money market account after your credit cards are paid off, using your extra found money. Once your cards are paid off, you can increase it to $5,000.

Myth 8: The budgeting myth.

Again, many good financial advisors recommend you observe where you're spending your money and then budget so much each month, which allows you to set aside money to pay off the principal on your debts. Budgeting gives you a false sense of security, and there is usually nothing left at the end of the month. The secret of debt elimination is to automatically take 10% to 20% out of your bank account each month to pay off debt—as if it were a tax. I can guarantee you that, if you take 10% to 20% out each month and pay it toward debt, you still will be broke at the end of the month, just like you are now, except that you will be well on your way to becoming debt-free.

Myth 9: College-funding myth.

Many people recommend that you start funding your child's education early, so that you have enough when they're ready for school. They recommend 529 plans that are run by different states, which have high fees and are actively managed funds. The returns are not guaranteed and many times dismal. You also have less control over the money, which cannot be used for non-education purposes. Money in 529 plans count against you when applying for federal student aid. Also, if not used for college, you will owe tax on the money.

It is better to focus on debt reduction. When you're debt-free, you can easily fund your children's college education with cash. The best way to fund a college education is through creating your own Personal Bank, which will be discussed in the next chapters.

Myth 10: The "more money" myth.

I have heard so many people say, "If I just had more money...." When I first began coaching my clients on how to make more money, without first teaching them to get out of debt, they just got into larger amounts of debt and are now trapped in their large homes and large, high-stress lives. Making money is an important part of this game plan and will help you accelerate your goal of eliminating all debt and creating a stress-free life. Peace of mind comes when you know you, your family, and your legacy are financially secure.

Myth 11: Avoid-paying-taxes myth.

Many people lose money by trying different schemes to prevent paying taxes. You should want to pay more taxes than anyone else because it indicates you are making more money than anyone. Rely on your CPA. A good CPA will keep you honest and make sure you don't give more to the government than required.

Myth 12: Retirement myth.

The idea of retirement was created during the industrial age of the 20th century. Everyone would work hard 5 days a week, take two weeks of vacation a year and retire at the age of 65. At this time, you were supposed to enjoy all the hobbies, family events, and adventures you missed when you were young during your working days.

Neil Pasricha, in his excellent book *The Happiness Equation* says that the men and women in Okinawa live an average of seven years longer than Americans and have the longest disability-free life expectancy on earth. They do not even have a word for "retirement." Instead, they have the word *ikigai* (pronounced like "icky guy"), which roughly means "the reason you wake up in the morning." You can think of it as the thing that drives you most. Such things as the Social, Structure, Stimulation, and Story you get every day keeps you from doing your *ikigai*. Pasricha also states that retirement is a broken concept because it is based on three assumptions that aren't true: that we enjoy doing nothing instead of being productive, that we can afford to live well while earning no money for decades, and that we can afford to pay others to earn no money for decades. He says "Never Retire."

The problem is, most Americans do not understand how money works and the importance of getting out of debt early, allowing them more choices early in their life. Once you are debt-free, how much do you really need to earn or work to have a great life? You will have a job you love with more time off or find a new type of employment that allows you to live your life as you always wanted.

From that point, you are in continual retirement, and you will have something to do that adds meaning to you and to the world. You will not even need to touch your retirement nest egg because you will continue to earn money the rest of your life on your terms. You will create your own Personal Bank to store money safely, create wealth, and never worry about the government or other financial institutions controlling you and your money again. This is true freedom and a new type of retirement.

AVOIDING FINANCIAL MISTAKES

Warren Buffett said, "The first rule of investment is don't lose money. The second rule of investment is never forget rule number one."

The most important way to keep your wealth is never to make a big financial mistake. Big financial mistakes usually occur because of greed and ego. I have known numerous individuals who have lost their entire portfolio in a get-rich-quick scheme. Such schemes range from real estate deals to limited partnerships; they can take the form of just about anything else that sounds too good to be true. Remember, there is no free lunch.

When you have a systematic guide to get out of debt, increase your business profitability, and conservatively invest in the US market, then you will become economically free in a fairly short time. Why take a risk on anything else? If you just stick with the simple Dr. Ace's Financial Freedom philosophy of investing, you will never put your retirement money at risk. Here are some other financial mistakes you should avoid:

- **Not stopping to find out what makes you happy.** The things that really make me happy are very simple and cost almost nothing. If I had known this earlier at the deepest level, I would not have needed to drive myself so hard to be successful. This is why the process of writing a new story is so important. Write down what you want your average day to look like. What are the things that make you happy? (Do not include shopping!) What are the happiest times you have enjoyed in your life? When you know who you are, it is easy to save money. Usually the simplest and least-expensive things make you happy. Try to spend the least amount of money trying to figure out what makes you happy. Rent your way through the discovery process (for example, rent that lovely condo in the mountains rather than buy it). Most people live a life of high debt and stress because they spend money, hoping it will make them happy. I guarantee that more money or things will not give you peace or happiness.

- **Allowing our vanity and ego to ruin our lives** by creating an unconscious compulsion to enhance one's identity through association with and purchase of expensive items, e.g., jewelry, exotic cars, and luxury homes. Yet, rarely do these purchases satisfy the ego desires that make one feel different and special.

- **Lending money to friends and family.** If you lend money to friends or family, please realize there is a good possibility you will never be repaid. Often this has a negative impact on the relationship. If lending the money is meaningful to you, then consider simply giving it as a gift. Never co-sign a loan; in most cases, you will end up paying the loan. A co-signer is a fool with a pen.

- **Falling for get-rich-quick schemes and scams.** Never get involved in any investment that you do not completely understand. With this guide, you do not have to take risks. You already have it made. When you are asked to invest in something new, just tell them that you invest only in no-load S&P 500 or the US stock market, but thanks anyway.

- **Listening to investment financial advisers** who say they can beat the market. Only a fool would say they can beat the market, so just stick with a no-load S&P 500 or total US market index fund that you can buy yourself from Schwab or Vanguard.

- **Getting into a limited partnership.** You lose control as a limited partner and are the last to be paid. Stay away from any investment or arrangement that you do not understand thoroughly or over which you do not have personal control regarding decisions.

- **Living in a high-cost, high-congestion, and high-tax area.** If you choose to work and live in a large city like San Francisco or New York City, where homes can be two to three times more expensive, you will find that traffic is terrible and that there are high state and city taxes that can delay your becoming debt-free and financially free. Think about moving to a tax-free state such as Texas, Florida, Wyoming, Washington, Alaska, New Hampshire, South Dakota, Tennessee, or Nevada. Live in a smaller, less-expensive, and safer community, and be able to buy a nicer and bigger home that you can pay off in five to seven years.

- **Buying too big a house.** Consider what you really need. Buying a bigger house than you need wastes money monthly. The cost of your home should not exceed 2.5 times your gross salary.

- **Buying a vacation home or large boat that you rarely use.** If this adds meaning to your life and you use it often, like more than sixty days a year, then it is worth the investment. That is, until it no longer adds meaning to your life—and at that time, you can sell it. It is not a bad idea for some properties like vacation homes or boats to be shared with other owners to dilute the expenses.

- **Buying timeshares.** Never buy them. You have a greater selection and a much lower price if you go to vacation rental by owner (VRBO.com).

- **Buying annuities.** Never buy them.

- **Starting another business** before you start making your own business successful. A well-run business can be very profitable. Maintain your focus, and start having fun again in your business.

- **Not marrying the right person, the first time.** Stay away from spenders. Find someone who is conservative in their spending habits and has financial goals like yours.

- **Not getting a prenuptial agreement if you have assets.** Get your spouse (male or female) to sign on the dotted line before you say, "I do."

- **Having too many "successful" marriages.** Before divorcing, try to reinvent your relationship and work through a counselor to see if you can make the relationship work. If there is no possibility of working it out, then you both deserve your freedom. There is often a lot of anger and trying to "get even" in the divorce process. I recommend you offer your spouse a generous settlement and treat her/him with kindness and respect. Always try to maintain strong relationships with your children; never put down your partner. If your spouse wants more and does not accept your generous offer, then tell your attorney that his or her job is simply to get you in front of the judge, and no longer communicate with your spouse's attorney. This will save both of you a lot money in attorney fees. Judges are normally fair in their settlements. If you continue to marry the same type of person (alcoholic, co-dependent, crazy), then this is the time for some personal growth and counseling.

Strategy 1

Double Your Money: Pay Off All Debts First

THE HIDDEN SECRET OF financial freedom is to pay off all debt first. This gives the highest rate of return guaranteed without taxes.

Banks, financial advisers, accountants, and Wall Street perpetuate the idea that debt is normal and that you would make more money by investing with them instead of paying off your house early. They also say that you will lose the tax benefit of writing off your mortgage interest. In most cases, this is not true but are the key reasons why people do not pay off their home and stay in debt. They perpetuate the lie that the extra principal payments toward your home does not earn you interest or make you money.

The truth is you can earn more than 200% interest by paying off the home early, as we see in the example below. They also state that the equity in your house is locked up and cannot be used. You can always use your home as collateral for any type of loan that you need. But, more importantly, you must see your paid-off home as a long-term bond that goes up with inflation and that your return on investment is the money that you did not have to use for your monthly payments to the bankers. Most importantly, how much do you really need to earn when you have no debt? This is all about your freedom and increased choice in your life.

Let us start with the big mortgage lie that the mortgage interest you pay makes you money by saving on your taxes. If you are in the 28% federal income tax bracket and you itemize your deductions, you will pay one dollar of mortgage interest and save 28 cents in taxes. This means you lose 72 cents for every 28 cents you save on taxes. For most families, the standard $24,000 deduction gives them a better tax result than itemizing to write off mortgage interest. So, the mortgage interest "write-off" benefit isn't really a benefit at all.

The next lie is that you are only paying 4.5% interest on your loan. Consider a $310,000 mortgage at 4.5% for 30 years. In the table below, you can see that, of the first year's loan payment (principal plus interest) of $18,849, only $5,001 goes to principal, and $13,848 goes to interest. This $13,848 that the bank keeps is lost to you forever. If you did not have a mortgage, what could you have used that money for? You think you have a 4.5% loan, but that year, it is actually 277% interest to the bank on your principal payment. At the same time, you are earning 0% interest from the bank on the money in your checking account. Does this seem fair?

Year	Interest	Principal	Balance
2021	$13,848	$5,001	$304,999
2022	$13,618	$5,231	$299,768
2023	$13,378	$5,471	$294,297
2024	$13,126	$5,722	$288,575
2025	$12,863	$5,985	$282,590
5-Yr Total	**$68,833**	**$27,410**	**$282,590**

Furthermore, in the 28% tax bracket, you had to earn around $17,724 and pay taxes on that to get $13,847 to give to the bank as interest payments. So that makes it a 354% interest-rate loan on your $5,001 principal payment. **The biggest loss is the $255,461 of things you could have bought** with the interest you paid the bank over the 30 years of the loan. These are the cars, vacations, college educations, home improvements, boats, and vacation homes gone forever.

You must understand that the interest is always the highest at the beginning of the loan. Over the first five years of the loan, you would have **paid $96,243** in loan payments and **only $27,410** would have gone to pay off the loan balance. For most loans, the first 10 years of this 30-year loan, the interest paid will always be above 100% of the principal paid. Always take advantage of this guaranteed high return!

If you invested an additional $5,231 (the second year's principal amount) toward the principal in the first year, you will have saved an entire year from your mortgage term, which means saving $13,618 in interest. That is a guaranteed 260% return without risk. With this great return, why would anyone leave money in their savings account, earning a miserable taxable 0.1%, when they could pay an additional principal payment on their home and earn a 260% tax-free return instead? To maximize your return, use the money from your saving and money-market accounts to accelerate debt payments. Many people get out of the market and sell all their non-tax-deferred stocks to pay off debts. **All extra payments must be directed only to the principal of the loan!**

When we have debt, saving money is an encoded trap that keeps us poor. In the above example, if you have $100,000 in your savings, taxable, or tax-deferred investments, the best, safest, and highest guaranteed return on that money would be to pay off debt. Paying $100,000 toward the $310,000 home mortgage would drop your mortgage to $210,000 and save you $121,360 in interest payments while paying off 13 years of the mortgage.

Compare this $121,360 made by paying off debt to the $200 you would get with a taxable .2% bank 3-month CD for the same $100,000. You must see the $100,000 put into the house as a high-return, safe, long-term, inflation-adjusted bond that is always available to you through lines of credit or second mortgages. Once the home is paid off, the money used for mortgage payments becomes a constant source of available cash flow. It is like getting money from a bond or rental property.

Here is another way to look at it. Your $310,000 home with interest over 30 years at 4.5% will cost you $565,000. If you are in a 28% tax bracket, you will have to have earned around $800,000 to pay for that $310,000. This is why we pay these mortgages off in 5 to 7 years.

Always pay off the loan in the shortest time period that you can afford. This will allow you to direct most of your payment to the principal of the loan instead of losing a majority of your monthly payment to lost interest which the bank keeps. If you get a 30-year loan with a 3.5% interest rate, your first year real interest rate will be 181%. If you can pay of the loan in 10 years, the real interest paid to the bank will only be initially 40% on that 3.5% interest rate and becomes less each year afterwards. If paid off in 5 years the 3.5% interest loan rate is only 17% initially. Look at the chart below. Check out: https://www.drcalculator .com/mortgage/old/

Loan first year real interest rates					
	30 year	**20 year**	**15 year**	**10 year**	**5 year**
Interest rate	**Real rate**	**Real rate**	**Real rate**	**Real rate**	**Real rate**
2.5%	109%	63%	44%	27%	12%
3.5%	181%	98%	66%	40%	17%
4%	225%	118%	79%	46%	20%
5%	337%	165%	107%	61%	25%
6%	486%	222%	139%	77%	31%
7%	686%	291%	176%	95%	37%
8%	954%	375%	219%	114%	44%

THE MORTGAGE INTEREST RATE CHALLENGE

Call up your bank or mortgage company, and ask them the amount of your mortgage payment that goes to principal and how much goes to interest this month. Divide the principal into the interest rate and multiply it by 100% to determine the true interest you are paying that month. (Interest/principal × 100% = real interest rate). **If you make one additional payment, this will be your rate of return on that investment.**

It is all about net worth. Our net worth is the total of all our assets, including our investments, bank accounts, and real estate, minus our debts. Paying off debt increases your net worth (wealth) and provides an asset that you can use in emergencies as loan collateral. Paying off debt is the safest and most powerful investment strategy. Learn to be happy with less tax deductions, especially when you can't even write off the mortgage interest due to the high standard deduction. Learn and avoid the tricks of the government and the banks to keep you in debt and servitude.

There is no good debt, only bad debt. All debt is bad, bad, bad! Debt keeps you imprisoned and prevents you from living a life of freedom, independence, and choice. Being overburdened with financial responsibilities increases your stress and can damage important and satisfying personal relationships and even lead to divorce, which could cost half of what you own. By changing your spending, saving, and investing habits, one step at a time, you can regain control of your life. You now know what interest payments really cost you and what to do to change your spending habits.

The advantages to paying off debt first are:

- Easiest and simplest to do and understand.

- No need for financial advisers and their expensive fees.

- It can give you a guaranteed 100% return on your money, without risk or taxes.

- Can be done automatically, right out of your bank account. You treat the payment as if it is a tax and becomes like a forced savings.

- Changes you from a spender into a saver.

- As you create equity in your home, you have access to cash through lines of credit or 2nd mortgages for opportunities or emergencies.

- Complete peace of mind and choices in your life because no one (banks) owns you.

- Once debt-free, it takes very little to live on. Now you have three times the amount of disposable income (previously, ⅔ of your disposable income was paid toward debt) to fund your own Personal Bank to have money to spend, invest, or just enjoy life with.

- Once your home is paid off, it acts like a long-term, inflation-adjusted bond. The 20% of your income that you were using to pay off your mortgage you now get to keep as a constant source of income that you never have to earn, and you will never have to worry about a house payment again.

DEBT IS THE DEVIL

When you become debt-free, there is no need to worry about your credit report because you pay cash for all your purchases. The ability to obtain credit is what got you into trouble in the first place. The idea that you need to build up your credit by borrowing is an illusion that keeps you in debt. But once you become debt-free, no one owns you, and this is true freedom.

Once debt-free, an individual would be able to maintain their lifestyle, fund their retirement, need to work only three days a week, and still take off eight to twelve weeks a year, which I call retiring-in-business. They could create a beautiful story and business environment for themselves and their teams, and love going to the office knowing that they have plenty of time off to play and rejuvenate. Under those circumstances, why would you ever want to retire?

When this strategy is implemented correctly, you will have created an automatic investment program using your own Personal Bank to buy income-producing real estate or low-cost index funds, and you will not worry about the ups and downs of the market. You will learn how to "retire-in-business," which would allow you to work only two to three days a week, and take eight to twelve weeks of vacation a year. This comes from understanding the systems in business management and investing in yourself to learn these skills.

Strategy 2

Create a Financial Freedom Game Plan

FINANCIAL FREEDOM BEGINS with creating a step-by-step game plan to first evaluate and reduce your discretionary spending, find ways to make more money, and to focus this found income toward debt reduction. This will allow you to pay off all debt within 5 to 10 years. Stop all consumption debt. Most families in America are imprinted to use their credit cards and consume, whether they have the money to pay for something or not. If you do this, you typically pay high interest rates; this is not an effective way to manage your money.

Act Today. Declaring that you are seriously committed to getting out of debt is the first step to achieving personal wealth. Go through the steps below. All forms can be downloaded from DoctorAce.com. Sit down with your significant other: Both of you must be on board, knowing that this will strengthen your relationship, eliminate stress around money, and give you back

your freedom. Then read this book together, and set time aside
to do the following:

1. Add up your net worth, that is, everything you
    own, and then subtract everything you owe in
    the chart below.

Determine Your Net Worth			
Assets	**Amount**	**Liabilities**	**Amount**
Personal Cash (Bank)			
Business Cash (Bank)			
Taxable investments (stocks)			
Tax-deferred investments (IRA/401[k])			
Cash-value life insurance			
Gold/Silver			
Other			
Real estate		How much is owed	
Main home		How much is owed	
Vacation homes		How much is owed	
Rental property		How much is owed	
Business building		How much is owed	
Business value		How much is owed	
Automobiles/boat		How much is owed	
Personal property		How much is owed	
Pension (20x yearly amt)		School loans	
Social Security (value = 20x yearly amount)		Credit card debt	
Other Assets		Other debt	
Total assets $		Total liabilities $	
		Net worth $ (Assets Minus Liabilities)	

Write down your total household income.

Net income source (after taxes)	Earner A	Earner B
Salary (net, take-home pay)		
Part-time or self-employment income		
Home-based business income		
Investment income		
Social Security		
Pension		
Veteran's benefits		
Other		
Individual totals		
Total income of A and B		

2. Reduce your monthly expenses. List all your current monthly expenses in the "current" column below. In the "reduced" column, record the lowest amount you can reasonably spend on each item. Total up all "reduced" amounts at the bottom of column 3, and then subtract that amount from your total income. The resulting number is your maximum possible found debt-reduction money. Go through your credit-card receipts and checkbook, and add up all your monthly expenses. Use the list below. See where you can eliminate or reduce certain expenses. Those in bold letters are some of the best places to look for found money.

Monthly expenses	Current	Reduced
Retirement-plan contributions		
Going out for lunch at work		
Dining out (other than work lunches)		
Groceries (use coupons)		
Telephone (including cell phone)		

Heating fuel		
Water/sewer		
Electricity		
Car cost (fuel and maintenance)		
Parking, tolls, etc. (carpool or bus)		
Car #1 payment		
Car #2 payment		
Insurance—automobile (higher deductibles)		
Insurance—health (higher deductibles)		
Insurance—home (umbrella insurance)		
Insurance—other		
Home-equity loan payment		
Re-finance home mortgage (walk away)		
Other loan payment		
Child care		
Cable or satellite TV		
Movies		
DVD rental		
Other entertainment		
Sports (golf, fishing, etc.)		
Health club		
Lawn maintenance		
Laundry and dry cleaning		
Pet food and care		
Subscriptions		
Online computer services		
Credit card payment		
Credit card payment		
Credit card payment		
Christmas gifts		

College education for children		
Private schools		
Emergency fund		
Other savings		
Total reduced monthly expenses =		

Total income minus reduced monthly expenses = _____
(this is your *found debt-reduction money* used to accelerate your debt payments)

3. Develop a spending journal, and for a month, write down each purchase you make (except regularly scheduled bills). This includes incidentals such as coffee, parking, and other items less than a dollar. Use mint.com or download from DoctorAce.com.

Date	Item purchased	Cash	Credit	Check	Amount

Setting Your Debt-elimination Plan in Motion

To come up with an effective strategy for eliminating debt, it's important to have a clear sense of your monthly expenses and to determine how many of these expenses are payments on specific debts. Personal-finance software programs such as Mint.com or Microsoft Money can help you greatly in organizing this information on your computer.

First, write down all debts that you owe, along with the minimum payment for each debt, from the smallest to the largest (see below). We start with the smallest debt because we want to see results quickly, which helps us to continue the plan. Take 10% to 20% of what you make, and set up automatic payment through your bank, starting with the smallest debt. Once that's paid off, move on to the next debt. Continue this until all debt is paid off. You can write a check each month for the extra payment, but automatic payments are much more effective. ***Very important: All payments must be directed to the principal of the loan, not just to the loan.***

Once you have made a commitment toward financial freedom and debt reduction, it's important to act by freeing up money from unnecessary expenditures. Cut up all credit cards except one that you may need. Change your spending habits, and use only cash, checks, or debit card to buy things. Use the 48-hour rule. For any purchase greater than $100, wait 48 hours to see if you really want to purchase that product. Most times, you will not.

Give yourself a set amount to spend each month so you get the feeling of what this is like. As an experiment, don't do *any* shopping for one month except for food. You may go through an initial withdrawal period. Facing your fears will help you to become wealthy. The way to stop salespeople from trying to sell you something is to simply say, "I can't afford that." If they persist, simply repeat your answer.

While you're reducing expenditures, be sure not to make any major purchases, such as a new car or boat, remodeling or a new house. I have had many great boats in my life, but someone else always owned them. For most people, boats always require more money than the pleasure they produce.

Save unexpected extra money, tax returns, bonuses, and pay raises, and immediately use this "found money" to pay off your consumer debt. Look for areas in your expenses that you can reduce. Do not buy new cars. You can save thousands of dollars by buying a car that is two to five years old. You may want to consider taking a second job for a short period of time to help eliminate credit-card debt. Some couples live on one salary and invest the other. Quality of life is found in our relationships, the experience and the detail—not in the number of possessions we own. We need less to live on when we move from a materialistic life to one that is more inspirational and spiritual.

Other ideas for finding extra money.

- Stop funding retirement until debt free, except for matching contributions.
- Get rid of your emergency fund. Your paid-off credit card becomes your new emergency fund.
- Evaluate/reduce holiday gift giving.
- Check bank/credit-card statement.
- Stop smoking.
- Properly maintain your home and car.
- Never buy a brand-new car until debt free.
- Never finance beyond 36 months.
- Take advantage of "cheap," meaningful vacations.
- Don't buy tools/boats you don't often use—rent or borrow them.
- Conserve utility usage.
- Avoid "Retail Therapy."
- Learn to say "No" to kids.
- Think like Warren Buffet and send your children to public grade schools and high schools instead of private schools.
- Stop funding your children's education. Let them pay for college.
- Apply all bonuses and pay raises toward debt.
- Eliminate private mortgage insurance (PMI) by paying down the mortgage balance to 80% of the home's original appraised value.

- Evaluate your real insurance needs.

- Auto insurance: get higher deductibles.

- Personal-liability insurance.

- Medical insurance.

- Get higher deductibles.

- Get an umbrella attachment.

- Never buy extended warranties.

- Use coupons (retailmenot.com, Joinhoney.com).

- Stop getting tax refunds.

- Spare-change jar.

- Have only a cell phone.

- Minimize dining out. Move to brown-bag lunches.

- Simplified lifestyle.

- Entertainment.

- Movies.

- Get rid of cable.

- Shop at outlet malls/Goodwill.

- See if you can refinance your home at a lower rate without fees through Quicken loans or a local bank.

- Buy a duplex, and live in one side; use your renter payment to double your monthly mortgage payments. Look at trailer-park or prebuilt homes as a starter home.

One of the fastest ways to become debt free is to move to a cheaper location. The average US home costs $290,000. It is a lot easier to get out of debt if you buy your home in a location where the home prices are low, where the median home prices is

$134,000 such as in Memphis, Tennessee compared to San Jose, California, where the average home is $530,000.

This is *not* a no-spending plan; it is a managed-spending plan. I am not saying you can't spend any money on the things you want. But I *do* want you to be aware of the impact that each expenditure has on your ability to build your wealth. Most people can easily spend and live on half the amount they normally spend.

Financial freedom is just a mindset and a numbers game. Once your plan is implemented, you will be debt free in 5 to 7 years. You now can stop worrying and focus on each day and enjoy the process of life.

An extra job will accelerate your debt reduction. Here are some ideas on how to make more money.

- Make more at your job, and put it toward debt.
- Do consulting work from home.
- Teach over the internet through Zoom.
- Set up an eBay account and business.
- Learn how to create an online business at home.
- Go to clients at their home (bookkeepers, home cleaning or computer expert).
- Teach college at night.
- Check out internet on "work-at-home jobs" (watch out for scams).
- Multilevel marketing (e.g., Mary Kay) (watch out for scams).
- Go back to school to give you opportunities for a higher-paying job, and make all efforts to limit your student-loan debts.

- With an extra job, you could be debt free three years earlier.

Use the debt-elimination approach (described below) to pay off all debts within five to ten years. Read through the debt-elimination-approach description, and then fill out the debt form to see how long it will take you to pay off all debts by making a 10% or 20% payment toward debt each month. **Automation of the payments is the secret!** I am not a big fan of budgeting. If you are serious about getting out of debt, automatically take 10% or 20% out of your bank account each month as if it were a tax. Live on the rest.

Filling out the Debt-elimination Worksheet below.

Identify your debts, and record them on the Debt-elimination Worksheet below (you can go to Doctorace.com and download the worksheet). First, pay all small debts (less than $10,000) starting with the smallest. This "small debt" category includes credit-card debt, consumer debt, auto-loan balances and small student loans. Start with the smallest debt (no matter how high or low the interest), and then use the money from your *debt-reduction savings account* to pay it off first, while continuing to make the minimum payments on your other debts.

At the beginning, it's important to get momentum and see that you are making progress, so don't worry about the respective interest rates now. If the high credit-card interest rate on a larger debt bothers you, you can always call the company and successfully negotiate a lower rate or transfer your balance to another credit-card company with a lower rate.

Once you have paid off the first debt, you'll feel a sense of empowerment. Paying off that debt frees up additional money, which you add to your savings. Use this increased savings to pay down the next-smallest debt. Fill out the worksheet in pencil so that you can update it each month. This will help you keep on track and stay motivated.

As you pay down debt, you gain momentum and free up more money to pay off the next debt. The money that pays off these debts comes from increased income, reduced spending, and the extra money that becomes available as you pay off each debt. If you have money saved, do *not* use that money for early debt reduction for at least six months.

Below is an example of how we pay off debt.

First, determine what percentage of income you want to pay toward debt. If you and your spouse's average income is $72,000, you would divide this by 12 months, giving you $6,000; after taxes, that would be $5,000. 10% of this would be $500 per month.

The $500 (10%) will be paid each month to the principal of the top loan in the chart. First, add the $500 to the Visa card $30 payment, giving you $530 per month to pay toward that loan, which will be paid off in two months. When the Visa card is paid off, apply that $530 plus $32 to the next MasterCard loan, which will result in $562; it will take three months to pay off *that* loan. Your efforts will continue to eliminate all your debt. The debts will be paid off in seven years and four months, and you will have an extra $31,176 per year to invest, save, take vacations, send children through college, or work less.

$500 (10%) Paid Monthly to Principal of Top Loan in the Chart

Name of Debt	Total Balance (smallest to largest)	Monthly Payment	Accelerated Monthly Payment	Months to Pay Off
Visa Card	$1,000	$30	$530	2
MasterCard	$1,500	$32	$562	3
Department store	$2,000	$36	$598	4
Car 1	$9,200	$520	$1,118	9
Car 2	$14,300	$750	$1,868	8
Home equity loan	$26,000	$370	$2,238	12
Mortgage at 4.5%	$155,000	$860	$3,098	50
Totals	$209,000	$2,598 ($31,176/yr.)		88 months (7 yrs. 4 mo.)

Your Debt-elimination Worksheet:
Calculate Paying Off Your Debt
(Annual household income: $ _____)

(Average American debt is 2.5 times the
annual household income)

1. Determine your extra monthly payments: $_____
Try for 10% or more of your monthly take-home income. If you
have only a home mortgage, then you should add 20% to 30% of
your monthly take-home income.

2. Write down each debt in the first column below,
prioritizing each debt from smallest to largest. Do not be concerned about the interest rate.

**3. Using the debt-elimination approach, add your
accelerator margin to the smallest debt,** making this new
monthly payment. Put this in column 4. To determine when the
debt will be paid off, divide this amount into the total balance of

that debt by the new monthly payment in column 4, and put the number of months to pay off in column 5.

4. When this debt is paid off, add what used to be the monthly payment amount to the next smallest debt payment, and place that in column 4. Again, divide this amount into the total balance of that debt by your new monthly payment in column 4. Put the number of months to pay off in column 5.

5. Continue adding each paid-off debt's monthly payment amount to its accelerated monthly payment and rolling the total amount to the next debt.

6. Add up the months in column 5 to determine when all debts will be paid off.

Name of Debt	Total Balance	Monthly Payment	Accelerated Monthly Payment	Months to Pay Off
1	2	3	4	5
Totals				

Things to keep in mind about your debt-elimination plan:

- Use only minimum payments to maximize the debt-elimination process.
- Use only the principal and interest portion of your mortgage payment (not tax/insurance).

- Interest rates are not a big factor.
- Only non-recurring debts go into your debt-elimination plan.

Write and post your Financial Goals. I am taking 10% of my income and paying off my debts. In six months (date), I will use 20% of my income toward an extra payment on my debts. I will pay off all credit-card debt in one year (date), my car in two years (date), and my home in six years (date). Each month, review and challenge yourself to increase your debt reduction.

Develop a support group of either family or coworkers. Most families' money issues cause the greatest stress, and most do not understand how debt can keep a person in prison and take two thirds of their income throughout their lifetime. In my office, I created and presented to my team and their spouse a debt-reduction plan, which you will find at DoctorAce.com. In this program, I showed them how to pay off debt, including their home, within 10 years, thereby freeing up more money to invest in their retirement fund. I also showed them how to invest safely with little risk and higher returns. Within six years, I have four of my employees completely out of debt, including their home, and the others have a game plan to be debt free within the next 10 years. Lisa and her husband are an example, below.

The greatest gift that I gave them is not being out of debt; the greatest gift is that I changed them from spenders to savers. This has done much to eliminate the money issues that many families argue about. The only drawback to this plan is that three out of the four team members who are now out of debt did not need to work as much and either now work part time in my business or left the business to enjoy their hobbies, which can be profitable. I just bring more people in and get them out of debt. Here is an example of one of those team members.

Lisa's Story

Lisa was my chief clinical dental assistant and was incredible at her job. She had a hobby selling things on eBay. Surprisingly, she was making more than $50,000 a year in her hobby.

Her husband was making about $15 an hour on his physically demanding construction job. They decided to live on his income and focus everything she earned from their eBay business and her salary from my dental office toward debt reduction and paying off their houses. They owned two homes, and, within four years, they had paid off their mortgage, sold the other one and invested the profits into her eBay business. Once debt free, she created her own personal bank, putting in $30,000 per year. In 25 years, at age 65, she will have $1,250,000 in her Personal Bank and will have used the money throughout the years for travel, personal purchases, children's education, and investing in their business. She will also have access to that money tax free for retirement.

Lisa has since left my dental practice. She and her husband work about fifteen to twenty hours a week on their eBay business and have plenty of time for travel and enjoying the adventures of life. They had their first child in November. It is surprising how, with strong intent, becoming debt free happens very quickly.

Continue to read books such as those found in this book's references section, and listen to audios about debt reduction, including the ones found at DoctorAce.com.

Become the teacher. First set up and start the program yourself. Bring your family and friends together and watch these videos. Pass out the handouts, and help them set up the program for themselves. Share other debt-reduction resources with them. Share this material within your community and help them regain their freedom.

Celebrate Success.

This is *not* a no-spending plan; it is a managed-spending plan. I am not saying you can't spend any money on the things you want...But I *do* want you to be aware of the impact that each expenditure has on your ability to build your wealth. Most people can easily spend and live on half the amount they normally spend.

Managing bumps in the road. If you have an emergency during this time—for example, major car repairs or unexpected medical bills—you can use your paid-off credit card or skip a month or two of debt-reduction payments and use the cash that would have gone toward debts to cover the emergency. The same is true if you feel you need an inexpensive vacation: skip a month or two of debt reduction, and pay for your vacation with cash. Just be sure to get back on track with your debt-reduction plan as soon as you can. I do *not* believe that you must have an emergency fund for you to start debt reduction. Some consultants recommend three to six months of income, but if you wait for that, it might take you two or three years to start your debt-reduction program. Once you have a paid-off credit card, you *do* have an emergency fund.

As soon as you have paid off all your small debts (less than $10,000), celebrate! Now take the "found money" you have freed up and use it to pay off large debts (more than $10,000), such as your car loan, your home mortgage, and any lines of credit. This may seem like a slow process, but once you've paid off all your debts and are regularly investing in your retirement funds, you'll have a considerable amount of excess money left each month to invest in the investment strategies described later in this book. By following this plan, most people can pay off all their credit-card debt in one year and their car in the second year. By the third year, they are making extra payments toward the principal on their mortgage. Most people following this plan can be debt free and pay off their home in seven to ten years.

When your last debt (home) is paid off, 40% to 60% of your income will be available for investments or to place into your **Personal Bank** (PersonalBank4U.com). This will allow you to become totally financially free in another eight or nine years.

Strategy 3

Learn How to Invest Safely and Simply

THE SECRET AND SIMPLICITY of this plan is that investing requires no decision-making until you become near financially free. Initially, all investment of your money goes automatically to pay off debt and then to create your own Personal Bank. The best, safest, and greatest return on your investment always comes from paying off debt first and by making more money at your work or business. The next safest and guaranteed investment is in the creation of a Personal Bank. This is a specialized, high-cash-value, whole-life insurance policy that gives you a consistent tax-free return. This is the gold standard in safe and predictable investing and will be discussed in chapter 5. Investing in the stock market may provide a higher taxable return but is not guaranteed, and is more volatile, with higher risks. Stock-market returns can be significantly increased when you learn to eliminate fees by investing on your own through a company such as Schwab or Vanguard, which I will discuss below.

Disclaimer

I have found the following investment information
to be helpful. I am not engaged in rendering professional services. If you require personal assistance or
advice, seek a competent professional. I specifically
disclaim any responsibility for any loss, liability
or risk, personal or otherwise, which is incurred
directly or indirectly from the use and application
of the contents of this book.

Many individuals get confused with investing and do not
understand how easy it is to invest on their own through a company like Schwab or Vanguard. That is why they are so vulnerable to investment schemes and high-fee advisers and brokers.
We seem to have an infinite capacity to stress ourselves and do
stupid things, especially when it comes to money. To a large
degree, this comes from greed and ego. I knew one individual
who took his entire retirement plan of $300,000 and put it into
a limited partnership. He did not really understand the potential
risks and rewards, and he had no control over them. Within one
year, he'd lost his entire retirement nest egg that had taken him
twenty years to earn. I know a very smart and skilled doctor
who got involved in a "Bernie Madoff"-type scheme and lost his
entire savings of $1.3 million that had taken him twenty years
to accumulate.

Debt reduction and financial freedom are important and can
be achieved quickly following this game plan. Most individual
investors rely upon money managers, advisers, and brokers who
engage in hyperactive trading to try to beat the market by picking
winners and timing the market. This is a losing strategy. In most
cases, investors would be better off consistently investing in index
funds like the S&P 500. Jack Bogle, founder of the Vanguard
group, believes in index funds and says actively managed funds

are a big scam. When you invest in loaded, actively managed mutual funds, you put up 100% of the capital and take 100% of the risk, and if you make money, they take up to 70% or more of the upside in fees. And if you lose money, they still get paid. They are charging you 10 to 30 times what it would cost for you to buy a low-cost index fund that would match the market and beat 96% of the mutual funds. Because fees are the enemy of the individual investor, we need to stay away from financial advisers and brokers who work on commission and thus put us into actively managed funds.

The problem is many CPAs, brokers, and financial advisors tell you not to pay off debt but to invest your money in the stock market through tax-deferred, government-controlled 401(k)s and IRAs. They put their clients' assets into actively managed mutual funds that took 3% to 4% of their return for themselves, resulting in a 60% to 70% loss of return that could have been made for my clients. The losses were in the millions of dollars in my clients' investment portfolios, thus preventing geometric progression of their retirement plans and undermining my advice.

Many of the "helpers" (brokers, mutual-fund companies, and financial advisors that you may have now) provide complicated investing strategies with multiple investment choices or investment theories such as Modern Portfolio Design, so you will think that investing is complicated and too hard for you to do alone. That is why investors are tricked into paying them high fees, even though their returns are less than the S&P 500 or US stock index. William Bernstein said, *"You are engaged in a life-and-death struggle with the financial service industry. Every dollar in fees, expenses, and spreads you pay them comes directly out of your pocket. Act as if every broker, insurance salesman, mutual-fund salesperson, and financial adviser you encounter is a hardened criminal, and stick to low-cost index funds, and you'll just do fine."* So, don't fall for that scam.

A good friend of mine recently married a beautiful lady whose husband had died three years before. She related a story of a broker she went to for help with her investments, which she knew little about. She was still dazed and confused from her loss and took all the funds she had gathered from selling homes, cars, and businesses, and closing accounts. In December 2012, she gave the broker all her assets and asked him to "Manage this, be conservative, thank you."

He immediately placed her in an "actively managed account" and charged a 1% "wrap fee" annually. *Plus*, there were fees inside the account, e.g., front-end loads on mutual funds and high annual fees on mutual funds! In mid-2014, my friend and his new wife tried to get a handle on her returns, fees, and commissions. They asked the financial adviser three questions: What was the return in the managed portfolio in 2013? (Answer .... +5%.) What was the S&P 500 return for 2013? (The answer was ... +32.31%.) The third question was: How much were the total fees charged to manage the portfolio for 2013? (The answer .... $28,000!) This story is not uncommon in the brokerage world and demonstrates why we need to understand the simple concepts of investing safely.

Here is an example from one of my clients who had more than $1.6 million that was managed by a large brokerage firm. Over a six-year period, his portfolio would have built *$863,881 more in assets* if it had been placed into a Schwab S&P 500 fund. Compare your portfolio to the S&P 500 and see how you do. Go to Doctorace.com for more videos and audios, and download and fill out the Excel comparison sheet seen below. Remember, the S&P 500 fund performs better than 96% of all other managed funds, and I have yet to see any of my clients whose portfolio has done better than the S&P 500 index fund. In most cases, they have lost significant amounts of money when they let the experts invest for them.

	Schwab S&P 500 mutual fund index annual return	Brokerage **trust** account	annual % return	**Loss**	Brokerage **401K** account	annual % return	**Loss**
Ticker sym	SWPPX						
Fees	0.03%		1%				
Cost/1M$	$300		$10,000				
Stocks/Bonds	100%/0		100%/0				
Invested		Opening balance			Opening balance		
2017	21.80%	$406,560	12.00%	($39,843)	$1,276,633	9.50%	($157,026)
2016	12.0%	$321,784	6.5%	($17,698)	$1,099,332	1.27%	($117,958)
2015	1.4%	$316,367	-2.3%	($11,706)	$1,262,352	-2.28%	($46,455)
2014	13.7%	$302,687	4.5%	($27,847)	$1,322,966	6.29%	($98,032)
2013	32.4%	$356,161	7.9%	($87,259)	$1,186,118	11.37%	($249,441)
2012	16.0%	$272,222	12.1%	($10,617)		Loss	($668,911)
			Loss	($194,970)			
						Total Loss	**($863,881)**

If you are with a financial advisor or a mutual-fund company that is charging you more than $1,000 to $4,000 per year, you are paying too much and should transfer assets to Schwab or Vanguard into a low-cost index fund. Remember that a 1% to 2% fee could reduce your retirement assets to the point that you will have to work another ten to fifteen years. I personally use Schwab because they are open 24 hours a day, seven days a week, have no minimum balance to open an account, and all trades within their funds and ETFs are free. Both Schwab and Vanguard make it very easy for you to transfer assets from your overpriced mutual-fund company and adviser into their company.

Most of us do not like confrontation with our past adviser when we try to transfer our assets. It becomes very easy when you call a Schwab representative and fill out the forms to have your assets automatically transferred into your new Schwab account. You don't even need to talk to your former adviser. To avoid the higher fees in your old company when you sell a stock or heavily loaded mutual fund, have the assets transferred to Schwab first; then sell them. There may be a few mutual funds that they cannot transfer over; those will need to be sold into cash at your former brokerage house.

You must understand that when you are in the stock market, you are gambling. When you are debt-free and have money stored in your own Personal Bank, you will never need to take risks in the stock market. But if you need a gambling fund (not more than 10% of your liquid assets) and you want to put it into the stock market and then invest on your own in an indexed Schwab or Vanguard S&P 500 fund or the total US stock market fund. You will do better than 96% of all actively managed funds.

Problems with tax-deferred retirement plans such as 401(k)s and IRAs.

You will be encouraged by all financial advisers to invest in the stock market through a 401(k). There are many problems associated with 401(k)s, including **High Taxes, Fees, and Risk.** Your money is locked up like in a prison, where access to your money without penalty until you are 59½ years old. The returns on your investments are not guaranteed, and the risk causes anxiety and frustration from your money being invested in the stock-market casino. You cannot even write off losses. You will eventually have to pay taxes when you withdraw from your account, and most people believe the taxes will be higher later than they are now. One of the biggest problems are all the fees of 2% to 3% you pay to your advisers and mutual-fund companies, who can take 50 to 70% of your return in compounded fees. The government can change the rules at any time. As an owner, you will have to spend time on administrating the plan and be responsible for all initial setup fees (IRS & Administrator), Annual administrative fees ($2000/year), IRS compliance fees ($150–$1000), high 401(k) fees, cost, and expense to close the plan (which may or may not be approved by the IRS). I have yet to see any plan make more than 2% to 5% annual return for the business owner. And taken out in retirement years, every dollar in the plan is taxed.

Instead of investing in a 401(k), I recommend that you create your own **Personal Bank,** where the returns are guaranteed for life and provides predictable tax-deferred growth and tax-free retirement income—with no luck, skill, or guesswork required. There is no volatility in your account—you have complete control and access to all your money. Your principal and growth are locked in, and you never lose money. It's not subject to market risks. You can access your money without government penalties or restrictions on how much income you can take or when you can take it. You can access your principal and growth with no taxes due, under current tax law. Your cash value can easily and immediately be tapped for any purpose at all, and your plan can continue growing as though you never touched a dime of it.

If you do have a 401(k) plan, you need to check fees because fees can significantly reduce what your retirement nest egg will be. I recommend you go to the website and use the company's free online Fee Checker tool at www.ShowMeTheFees.com. Once fees are compared, many people move their plans to America's Best 401(k).

As an example, one of my clients who had about $1.4 million in her plan and added about $100,000 each year did a fee comparison. America's Best 401(k) total annual investment-related fees were 0.5%, compared to 1.73% in her original plan. If both plans got a 7% return over the next twenty years, the 1.23% difference in fees would have cost her $1.7 million in lost retirement savings for herself and her employees. To look at this in another way, **because of that 1.23% fee, which would have resulted in a $1.7 million personal financial loss**, she and her employees would have to work for another ten years before retiring. Over a 30-year period, the loss would be $4.93 million. How many more years do you have to work with a 3% adviser or actively managed fund fee? By eliminating the fees, it allows you to buy back the one thing that is limited in your life, which is your time on this planet. This is why it is essential that you compare plans. If you have a 401(k) or other IRAs in managed accounts, roll them over into a Schwab or Vanguard IRA account.

If you need to gamble and have more control of your money and less in taxes over time, stay away from tax-deferred accounts, and create an individual taxable account and invest (Gamble) with after-tax dollars. Because there are always ups and downs in the market, wait until after there is at least a 10% drop in the market before you buy. If the market drops more, continue to buy. You can buy the Schwab S&P 500 index mutual fund (ticker symbol SWPPX) at the expense ratio of 0.03%, or the Vanguard 500 index mutual fund (ticker symbol VFIAX) with an expense ratio of 0.04%. Or you can buy Schwab US Broad Total Market index mutual fund (ticker symbol SWTSX) at the expense ratio of 0.03%, or the Vanguard Total Stock Market Index mutual fund (ticker symbol VTSAX), with an expense ratio of 0.04%. That's it—you're done. Now enjoy your life.

The secret of this game plan is to make more money at work or in your business and focus all money toward debt reduction. Once you are debt free, your assets, such as your business or your home, act like a long-term, inflation-adjusted bond that can be used to obtain a line of credit or as a source of income. The next safest form of investment is creating a Personal Bank. This is a specially designed, dividend-paying high-cash-value whole-life insurance policy, where 87% of your premiums go into cash value with a small term rider that accelerates the growth in the policy. The modified policy reduces the commission the adviser receives by 70% to 85%, and you will have up to 90 times more cash value, especially in the early years, than with a traditional whole-life policy. Because of the lower commission, less than 2% of insurance agents know about or offer this policy. To find an agent who knows how to design a high-cash-value policy with the right companies, check out the links at PersonalBank4u.com.

These policies offer guaranteed tax-free growth and safety for your principal investment regardless of the ups and downs of the stock market or the economy. You will be able to use it as a financial-management tool right from the beginning. This policy provides you tax-free access to your money for purchases, disability income or tax-free money for your retirement years, giving you guaranteed growth. It provides peace of mind and an income-tax-free legacy that you can pass on to your loved ones and/or favorite charities without going through probate. This is one of the safest, no-risk investments and acts like a pension or long-term bond. Because of their safety, consistent returns, and the liquidity, most major banks have cash-value life insurance on their senior executives and is their tier-1 asset on their balance sheet.

Strategy 4

Create a Personal Bank

NOW THAT YOU ARE debt-free and have $20,000 to $100,000 a year available to invest, where should you put your money?

Now is the time to create your own Personal Bank that gives you control of your finances for the rest of your life. What is a Personal Bank? We are not really starting an actual bank but using the financing facility of a whole-life insurance contract to function like a bank for us. The infinite-banking concept was created by by Nelson Nash in the 1980s. It has also been known as Private Family Bank, Bank on Yourself, Infinite Banking, or High-Cash-Value, Whole-Life Insurance. It uses a specially designed high-cash-value, whole-life insurance policy that maximizes cash value in the policy enabling you to store your money safely while receiving a tax-free 4% to 6% return. Plus, it provides a death benefit for your family. Like a savings account, the cash value in the policy can be used and accessed at any time for any reason. This option is for everyone but especially for those who are fearful of the risks and the volatility of the stock market. The main purpose of your own Personal Bank is to provide a place to save money while receiving a high tax-free yield, build wealth, and create a consistent stream of income to invest and to use for retirement. When debt free, you need a place to keep your wealth tax free and never have a need to borrow from a bank again because now you can borrow from your own Personal Bank.

Many Americans feel that whole-life insurance is riddled with high commissions and fees that end up hurting the investor. This is true with traditional whole life insurance policies, where the insurance agent gets almost 100% of the first year's premiums and takes three years to have any cash value in the insurance policy. A properly designed policy creates high cash value and not high commissions. These modified policies put nearly 90% into cash value the first year and only 10% pays for the basic insurance policy. The cash value in these policies is tax deferred and can be taken out tax free during retirement years. The insurance agent's commission is reduced by 90%. In a policy where $10,000 is put into the policy for 30 years, the total commission for the agent could be as low as $1,420 depending on the company. Compare this to investing the same $10,000 in a mutual fund returning 7%. A 1% adviser fee results in a $200,485 commission over the same 30 years. If the mutual-fund company gets an additional 1% fee, the total commission will be $359,580 commission and a 3% fee, which is not unusual, will give your adviser and mutual-fund company $486,296 in commission. If you invested $100,000 per year, you will give them as much as $4,862,960 over the 30 years, and 96% will not even beat the S&P500 index fund. The late John Bogle said, in *Market Watch,* "If you pay a hefty fee to an active manager, what happens to your potential return? Answer: Nothing good. At 2.5%, over a typical investor's lifetime, an astounding 80% of compounding returns ends up in the hands of the manager, not the investor." Additionally, you will have to pay capital gains tax or 30% to 45% personal tax on all 401(k) withdrawals and will not have the advantage of an income-tax-free death benefit associated with high-cash-value, whole-life insurance.

Dave Ramsey, a nationally known speaker on eliminating debt early, is not a strong proponent of whole-life insurance. The whole-life insurance he is talking about is sold by those 99% of agents who do not use infinite-banking concepts. He brings up the argument that, when you die, you get only the death benefit and none of the cash value inside the policy. What he does not understand is that the death benefit increases over time, so, at death, the death benefit is higher than the initial death benefit and cash value combined. See example 3 in the chart below where the death benefits started at $572,260, and at 20 years, the cash value is $661,086, and the death benefit is $1,533,049. You have $960,789 more in the policy than the original death benefit and more than the cash value. If you were in a term policy that provided $500,000 in death benefit at the end of 20 years, it would only be $500,000. Another way to look at this is if you sold your $500,000 home; if you had $200,000 in equity in the home, you would only get the $500,000 and not the extra $200,000 in equity. Dave Ramsey also states that none of his financial experts and advisers recommend whole-life policies and believe it is the worst investment you can make. The main reason for this is that none of these financial experts and advisers ever make a dime on the money you use to buy a whole-life policy.

Creating your own Personal Bank would entail working with a life-insurance agent who meets specific criteria. This agent must know how to design a whole-life insurance policy that maximizes cash value and satisfies the IRS's non-MEC requirements. To maximize cash in the policy, they should work only with dividend-paying mutual-insurance companies, such as Mass Mutual, Guardian, New York Life, and Northwestern Mutual. These 4 major mutual companies all have a current guaranteed rate of 4% and pay the surplus of dividends in addition. The guaranteed rate plus the dividend surplus equals your annual tax-deferred rate of return. The top 4 companies' dividends for 2019 were between 5.00% and 6.40%. These companies have always paid a dividend for the 160+ years they've been around. Mass Mutual and Guardian have more flexibility, are easier to work with, and have fewer loopholes. Some smaller companies, such as Lafayette Life, Penn Mutual, Mutual Trust, Security Mutual, Ohio National, and several others are highly rated. Make sure that the agent knows how to design your policy so that only 10% of total contribution is allocated toward the insurance premium (death benefit), and the remainder is allocated toward a small term rider and the cash value in the policy.

These life-insurance companies are "mutually owned" so that you participate in the company's profits and dividends at the end of the year. Correctly designed policies maximize your cash accumulation by putting 10% of your premium toward death benefits and 90% toward cash value and small term rider. This reduces an agent's commission by 70% to 90% but maximizes your policy benefits.

The big difference in whole-life policies' design: The majority of whole-life policies sold and designed today put 100% of the premium toward death benefit the first year, with nothing going to cash value. When you create your own Personal Bank, you want 90% of the premium to go to cash value (PUA—paid up additions) and only 10% directed toward the death benefit. This policy is about high cash value and not high commissions. The illustration below compares three whole-life policies. In example 1, 100% of premium goes to death benefit. Example 2 is designed so 40% goes to death benefit, and 60% goes to cash value. Example 3 is designed for maximum efficiency, where 10% goes toward death benefit, and 90% goes toward cash value, which you can use immediately. Example 1 has no cash value until year 3, and it takes 11 years to catch up with the money you invested into the policy. Example 2 is a little better, but it still takes eight years to catch up. In example 3, almost 90% of your money is in cash value the first year, and somewhere between year 4 and 5, you catch up to the money you put into the policy. After 20 years, example 3, with the 10/90 ratio has the most cash value and the highest death benefit compared to the other two examples. In policy year 21 you see a significant drop in death benefit in example 1 and 2 because we executed what's called a reduced paid-up option which eliminates the base premium all together and have the policy premium paid through dividends and interest. By doing so we forfeit the right to pay money into the policy. This causes a significant drop in death benefit especially in policy where most of the premium was focused on death benefit such as in example 1 and 2. We see no drop in example 3 death benefit. Many insurance agents who understand and present the infinite-banking concept recommend that you put 40% toward death benefit and 60% toward cash value, which gives them a bigger commission. These agents may also be able to offer a 10/90 option if asked. If not, find an agent who can design a policy that meets the above requirements and can provide you with 10% going to death benefit and 90% toward cash value. Find these agents at PersonalBank4U,com.

The policy's primary use is to hold and build cash in a guaranteed tax-deferred 4% to 5% return safe environment, to be used for future investments, with the death benefit being secondary. The life-insurance policy gives you more safety, liquidity, flexibility, and control of your money than any savings vehicle or retirement plan you will own. For more than a century, whole-life insurance has been used by major banks, Fortune 500 Companies, and the wealthy and is often their tier 1 safest asset. Financial institutions, corporations, and banks buy life insurance by the billions and use it for many different reasons. Not only does it increase their financial stability and reduce their taxes, it is an ideal place to fund employee pensions, healthcare costs, and other benefits.

The cash value in the policy grows tax deferred, and all money borrowed from the policy is tax-free. You earn a guaranteed

Yr	Age	Example 1			Example 2		Example 3	
		100% to Death Benefit (DB)			40% DB/60% Cash Value		10% DB/90% Cash Value	
		Annual Outlay	Cash Value	Death Benefit	Cash Value	Death Benefit	Cash Value	Death Benefit
1	41	$20,000	$0	$1,350,711	$11,470	$965,598	$17,309	$572,260
2	42	$20,000	$0	$1,350,711	$23,511	$1,005,527	$35,501	$626,710
3	43	$20,000	$18,275	$1,361,509	$43,293	$1,044,824	$56,303	$680,297
4	44	$20,000	$40,313	$1,373,166	$65,218	$1,083,547	$78,463	$733,100
5	45	$20,000	$63,368	$1,385,932	$88,227	$1,121,756	**$101,760**	$785,204
6	46	$20,000	$87,473	$1,399,727	$112,352	$1,159,527	$126,228	$836,709
7	47	$20,000	$112,496	$1,413,880	$137,562	$1,196,921	$151,903	$887,701
8	48	$20,000	$138,460	$1,428,394	**$163,910**	$1,233,981	$178,856	$938,238
9	49	$20,000	$165,429	$1,442,848	$191,461	$1,270,771	$207,149	$988,406
10	50	$20,000	$193,445	$1,457,363	$220,261	$1,307,236	$236,846	$1,038,131
11	51	$20,000	**$222,503**	$1,471,844	$250,376	$1,343,404	$268,044	$1,087,451
12	52	$20,000	$252,551	$1,486,311	$281,806	$1,379,386	$300,767	$1,136,517
13	53	$20,000	$283,624	$1,501,009	$314,643	$1,415,206	$335,109	$1,185,363
14	54	$20,000	$315,812	$1,516,153	$348,930	$1,450,986	$371,126	$1,234,153

			Example 1		Example 2		Example 3	
			100% to Death Benefit (DB)		40% DB/60% Cash Value		10% DB/90% Cash Value	
Yr	Age	Annual Outlay	Cash Value	Death Benefit	Cash Value	Death Benefit	Cash Value	Death Benefit
15	55	$20,000	$349,148	$1,532,007	$384,741	$1,486,769	$408,923	$1,282,948
16	56	$20,000	$383,329	$1,552,516	$422,046	$1,522,707	$448,577	$1,331,955
17	57	$20,000	$420,332	$1,577,529	$461,686	$1,558,885	$490,375	$1,381,289
18	58	$20,000	$460,327	$1,606,958	$503,766	$1,595,335	$534,382	$1,430,994
19	59	$20,000	$503,470	$1,640,282	$548,414	$1,632,094	$580,713	$1,481,119
20	60	$20,000	$549,925	$1,677,562	$595,774	$1,669,031	$629,481	$1,531,488
21	**61**	**$0**	**$578,585**	**$1,182,041**	**$626,825**	**$1,280,593**	**$661,086**	**$1,533,049**
25	65	$0	$708,367	$1,298,779	$767,430	$1,407,070	$803,507	$1,548,608
30	70	$0	$909,369	$1,474,286	$985,196	$1,597,219	$1,030,668	$1,670,938
35	75	$0	$1,161,494	$1,683,861	$1,258,349	$1,824,276	$1,316,068	$1,907,954
40	80	$0	$1,469,696	$1,934,320	$1,592,257	$2,095,626	$1,666,155	$2,192,886
50	90	$0	$2,252,336	$2,589,784	$2,440,171	$2,805,761	$2,560,830	$2,944,498
60	100	$0	$3,324,817	$3,324,817	$3,602,101	$3,602,101	$3,791,455	$3,791,455

tax-free 4% to 5% each year, including dividends. Growth inside an insurance policy is called a "dividend" and is considered a "return of premium." Since they are considering it a return of what you have already paid, it is not taxable. This is what the average stock investor earns each year, except that the returns from your Personal Bank are tax free under current law. Within the first year, more than 85% of the premiums are now available as cash value. On average, after 3 to 5 years, all your premiums paid are available in cash value. Money can be retrieved from your account for any reason through a loan process without any application or approval by using your cash value as collateral. You borrow from the company's general fund at a 5% interest rate. Because you borrow the money from the insurance company's general fund, all cash value in your policy continues to grow at around 5%, which is as good as a free loan.

Your Personal Bank as a financing tool.

The unique and powerful advantage of your Personal Bank is that it allows you to continue to grow your money at the same rate regardless of any loans you take. The interest that you have been giving to your local bank and credit-card companies through car purchases, vacations, home mortgages, equity lines of credit, and student loans is a huge, wealth-draining loss for you. When you borrow from your own Personal Bank, all the money and interest you pay goes directly back to you. You recapture the interest that you pay to banks and finance companies for the major items that you need during a lifetime. Every time you borrow from your insurance policy and repay the loan, you make more money than the interest you pay. Because many of your loans may be for business purposes, the interest portion of your repayment back into your policy may be tax deductible. Tax deductions may also apply to the interest to the loans you use for personal investments such

Yr	Age	Annual Outlay	Annual Dividend	Net Cash Value Growth	Cash Value	Annual Loan	Loan Repayment	Loan Interest	Loan Balance	Cash Value
1	46	$50,000	$0	-2,829	$47,171	$0	$0	$0	$0	$47,171
2	47	$50,000	$763	$75	$97,246	$0	$0	$0	$0	$97,246
3	48	$50,000	$1,577	$2,774	$150,020			$0	$0	$150,020
4	49	$50,000	$4,476	$5,310	$205,330	$0	$0	$0	$0	$205,330
5	50	$50,000	$5,103	$8,238	$263,568	$200,000	$0	$0	$200,000	$53,568
6	51		$6,034	$11,172	$247,740	$0	$50,000	$10,000	$160,000	$106,740
7	52		$5,076	$11,643	$286,383	$0	$50,000	$8,000	$118,000	$162,483
8	53		$5,282	$12,387	$298,770	$0	$50,000	$5,900	$73,900	$221,175
9	54		$5,564	$12,948	$311,718	$0	$50,000	$3,695	$27,595	$282,743
10	55		$5,872	$13,546	$325,264	$0	$28,975	$1,380	$0	$325,264

as real estate and startup businesses. Always check with your CPA concerning the specific tax interest deductions with these loans.

As an example (see illustration below), if you have $263,568 in cash value, you can borrow up to $200,000 from the company's general fund using your cash value as collateral. This leaves your cash value intact to continue to earn your 5% return on the full $263,568, as if you'd never touched it in the first place.

Over the next 5 years, you will have paid $28,975 in loan interest back to the insurance company. During those same years, your $263,568 in your cash value has grown to $325,264, earning you $61,696 in interest and dividends! In fact, the growth of your cash value has covered the $28,975 of loan interest and has given you a $32,731 profit. Note at year 10, you have the same $325,264 cash value as you'd have if you'd never taken out a loan. It is better to create a whole-life policy first and use the cash value in your policy to pay off debt instead of using cash. Even though the 5% interest is the same on the growth and the loan, you are always earning the 5% interest and dividends on an ever-increasing cash-value balance while the 5% you are paying on the loan is on a decreasing loan balance. Because you are borrowing the money and not withdrawing the money from your cash value, there are no taxes on the capital gains. During your retirement years, you can borrow money each year from your cash value tax-free and never pay it back. The interest and money you borrowed will be deducted from your death benefits.

When borrowing money from your policy, understand that there is a difference between non-direct-recognition and direct-recognition insurance companies. When you borrow from a non-direct-recognition company, they do not recognize that you borrowed money from your cash value and will continue to credit you the same dividends and interest as if you'd never taken out a loan. The loan interest on the borrowed money goes to the insurance company. The death benefit and cash value will be reduced by the loan payment until the loan is paid back. You will still earn their yearly dividend rate on the total cash value, and, when the loan is paid back, the death benefits and cash value are completely restored as if you'd never had taken a loan. Mass Mutual insurance is an example of a non-direct-recognition company.

With a direct-recognition company such as Guardian, you will receive their dividend rate on all money still in cash value. You will also receive a slightly different dividend on the money that is outstanding in policy loans, which closely matches the loan interest rate at that time. With some direct-recognition insurance companies, the dividend paid on the loan portion can be significantly lower than your loan interest rate. This is usually true with smaller companies, so always check with the agent to determine the true historical dividend paid on borrowed money. The main takeaway is that direct-recognition companies still pay a dividend on borrowed money but at different rates. Guardian insurance company is a direct-recognition company and currently pays a slightly higher dividend on borrowed money. Guardian also has an option to change your policy from a direct recognition to a non-direct recognition at year 10.

The question is "How much do you want to save?" This is a high-powered savings program with a death benefit. You must see the premiums not as bills but deposits into your cash-value savings account. So how big do you want your cash value (savings) to grow over time? The cash value is a combination of the premiums you pay and the interest and dividends that the policy earns each year. This creates an exponential growth curve.

Most life-insurance policies are sold on how cheaply they can provide a death benefit. They say that you should buy term insurance and invest the difference. The problem is that very few people invest the difference, and less than 1% of term policies' claims are paid, which means all that money put into term insurance is lost. This also means 99% drop their policy in their

60s because the premiums are too expensive and have no life insurance when they die, leaving nothing to their family at a time of greatest need. With a high-cash-value, whole-life insurance policy, you need to know how much premium you can put into the policy's cash value rather than into death benefit costs. The death benefit is a bonus, which will be in effect until your death, leaving an income-tax-free legacy for your family. The policy is designed to optimize cash-value accumulation, and then we will determine how much death benefit we will buy.

Because the policy is designed to increase the cash value, they add a paid-up addition (PUA) rider, which provides small amounts of death benefits through term insurance that enable them to significantly increase the cash value in a much higher ratio than the base policy can. The PUA rider allows for a large cash value in your policy. The insurance companies require that at least 10% of the premiums go into life insurance (death benefit). So, 10% of your premiums go to base whole-life policy and 90% goes to PUA's for cash value and a small term policy rider while making up 100% of your Personal Bank premium. Remember that the cash value grows tax free and can be accessed tax-free. That is why the tax-free 5% you are getting from your whole-life insurance policy is like an 8% return in the market, where you must pay capital gains taxes on your non-IRA accounts or personal income tax on withdrawals from your 401(k) plan. The comparable return may even be 9% to 10% in your Personal Bank when you consider the 2% to 4% loss in advisory or mutual-fund fees and the money lost buying term insurance.

In designing the plan, your agent must be knowledgeable about how much cash is built into the policy to ensure the policy is not classified as a modified endowment contract (MEC) based on the IRS Seven Pay rule. In 1988, the tax law changed because certain insurance policies funded cash value too rapidly and were classified as a modified endowment contract. The IRS eliminated the use of such policies as short-term tax-free savings vehicles by imposing stiff penalties. The IRS created the Seven Pay Test rule, in which the IRS limits the total amount you can pay into a policy in any consecutive seven years of its existence. This amount is compared to the sum of the net level premiums that could have been paid on a guaranteed seven-year pay whole-life policy providing the same death benefits. If you tried to put too many premium dollars in the cash value compared to the policy's death benefit, you have crossed the dreaded MEC line. To satisfy the MEC rule the death benefit is raised through a cheap term insurance rider allowing greater cash value in the policy.

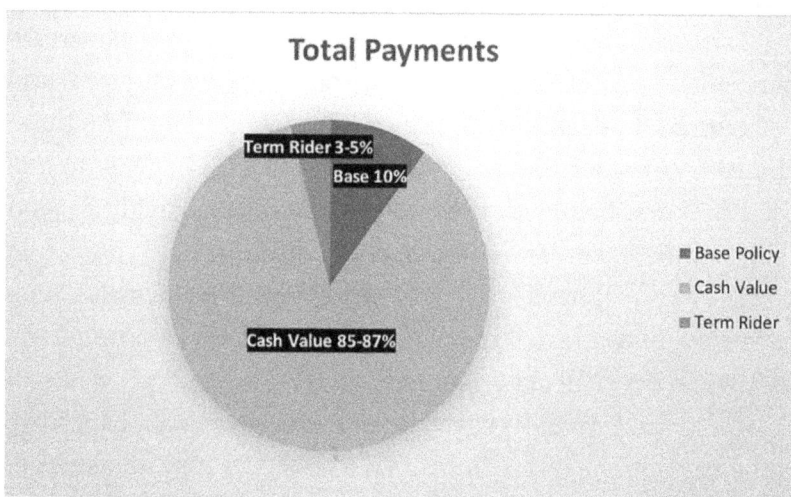

Total Payments

Term Rider 3-5%

Base 10%

Cash Value 85-87%

- Base Policy
- Cash Value
- Term Rider

Each policy needs to be custom designed to meet each person's individual long-term financial goals, your current financial needs, your current cash flow, your current savings, and your legacy needs.

You can also borrow money for your retirement out of these policies and not pay back the loans. The Personal Bank is more like a defined benefit plan, most often known as a pension, because it promises you a set payout when you retire. Because of costs, most employers have eliminated defined benefit plans and replaced them with defined contribution plans, like a 401(k) or 403(b). These plans place the burden of investing on the employee with no guarantee of investment returns or specific benefits when they retire. Your Personal Bank has many more advantages over a regular 401(k) plan. There are no restrictions like you find in qualified retirement plans such as minimum distributions, restrictions and penalties on withdrawal before age 59; all distributions are taxed at your personal tax rate. Your Personal Bank also allows you to make larger contributions than most traditional qualified plans. The growth in cash value is tax deferred; you can access your funds tax free, and you have a death benefit with all inheritance income going income tax free to your heirs.

The Personal Bank becomes your legacy, and you can create participating whole-life policies on yourself, your children, and your grandchildren and be the owner of each policy. As these children get older, the policies' cash value can be used to buy their first car, help with their college education, weddings, and their new business. The children repay these loans to your bank.

The Personal Bank is the ideal saving vehicle for your children's education. In contrast, if your child needs to take out a private loan, they will have to fill out a loan application. The application has all the income and credit-score requirements of any regular bank loan. If the student has no credit history, a co-signer may be required. The student or co-signer's FICO score determines the loan's interest rate. The co-signer is obligated for the loan's repayment. Repayment consistency affects the co-signer's FICO score. Compare this to a Personal Bank student-loan application, where there is no application process. You simply submit the loan amount to the insurance company and receive the money in about 5 business days.

Comparing a normal student-loan-repayment plan, the student must begin repaying most federal student loans right after s/he leaves college or drops below half-time enrollment, plus loans start repayment once the loan is fully disbursed (paid out). That can even be while the student is still in school. A Personal Bank student loan, on the other hand, can be paid back whenever you, the policy owner, choose.

Let's compare a 529 plan to using a Personal Bank. Withdrawals from a 529 plan are tax-free to the extent your child (or other account beneficiary) incurs Qualified Higher Education Expenses (QHEE) during the year. If you withdraw more than the QHEE, the excess is a non-qualified distribution. Whoever receives this non-qualified money will have to report taxable income and pay a 10% federal penalty tax on the earnings portion of the non-qualified distribution. You *cannot* include the following expenses: insurance, sports or club activity fees, and many other types of fees that may be charged to your students but are not required as a condition of enrollment. The expenses for a computer may not be included unless the institution requires that students have their own computers. Other costs that may not be included are transportation costs (like bringing your child home for the holidays), repayment of student loans, and room-and-board costs in excess of the amount the school includes in its "cost of attendance" figures for federal-financial-aid purposes.

529 plan contributions cannot exceed the amount necessary to provide for the qualified education expenses of the beneficiary. Be aware that there may be gift-tax consequences if your contributions, plus any other gifts, to a beneficiary exceed $14,000 during the year. A 529 account owned by a parent for a dependent student is reported on the federal-financial-aid application (FAFSA) as a parental asset. Any money remaining in a 529 account after education expenses are withdrawn is subject to standard qualified plan withdrawal and taxation rules. And, lest we forget, 529 plans are invested in mutual funds in the stock and bond markets, where values fluctuate and could be down when needed.

When the Personal Bank is used for education expenses, the policy owner alone decides what the money can be used for. There is no such thing as a non-qualified distribution. There are no penalties under any circumstances. There are no regulatory limits on, or tax consequences to, how much you put into a Personal Bank for funding a child's education. While it's true that, once a policy is underwritten, it is limited to that maximum funding level. However, you can start additional policies to add any amount you want to your savings. Money saved in a Personal Bank is not reported on applications for college financial aid. Money remaining in a Personal Bank policy after education expenses have been withdrawn, grows tax-free, can be taken out tax-free, and will pass on to the beneficiary tax-free.

Ownership of the policy can also be transferred to the student. When ownership in the policy is transferred, taxes are due on any gains but only to the new owner. Policy cash value always goes up, so there's no fear of market volatility when the money is needed. It's much simpler, more flexible, and less risky to pay for a child's or grandchild's education through a Personal Bank policy loan than through any typical student loan. Plus, it offers a powerful additional benefit that no student loan offers, which is the death benefit on the life of the person paying into the policy. The student can be designated as the beneficiary. A trust can be designated to control responsible use of the money. The main point here is, if you live and can fully fund the Personal Bank to pay for the child's education, it's paid for. If you die before you're able to save up enough, the death benefit will fund the child's education. This is better than any other savings plan.

It can get even better. Once the student's education is complete and they have a job, the policy owner can make them a life-changing offer. If the child makes loan payments and pays off the policy loan balance over time, the parent or grandparent can agree to transfer policy ownership to the child at that time. This will not only transfer control of the policy's cash value to the child, but teaches them the value of saving, the importance of getting out of debt, conservative safe investing, and help them implement a forced savings plan for their retirement. It provides them with a wealth-building system they can continue to profit from throughout their life. Even after this transfer, let's not forget that the death benefit is still active on the parent's or grandparent's life if the child continues making at least minimum premium payments. When the insured person eventually dies, the child will receive the death benefit with instructions how to use it to start Personal Banks for their children. This can provide an opportunity to start a generational wealth-building system that will make each generation potentially wealthier than its predecessors. You can create a financial-independence legacy for your family using your Personal Bank.

This is a permanent whole-life policy, in which your annual premiums never increase. In term-life and universal life insurance policies, the annual premiums increase as you get older, and eventually the cost of the premiums become unsustainable. This is why less than 1% of term policies and 20% of universal life policies are ever paid. Because this is a high-cash-value policy, you can choose to stop your premium payments after just a few years, allowing your premiums to be paid by the increasing growth of cash value from your guaranteed returns and dividends. If you do so, you will miss out on all that tax-deferred growth and tax-free income that you would have had by continuing to fund your policy.

One of the main purposes of your Personal Bank is to pay off your debts. Every dollar you use to eliminate your debts remains in your bank, accumulating interest and dividends even when you borrow from the policy to pay off debts. The cash value in the policy acts also as an emergency fund. At the end of the process, your debts are paid off, and all the dollars you used to do it with are still in your bank, continually growing. This is also one of the best options to transfer wealth and create a legacy for your children or grandchildren. The Personal Bank should be maximized before investing in the market because it has the following advantages:

- It is one of the safest investments, in which all growth is tax free and guaranteed.

- The Personal Bank provides a tax-free vehicle to safely put the excess money that becomes available when you become debt free, which is significantly higher than the limits that can be put on a retirement plan.

- Tax-free removes the uncertainty of what increased taxes could do to your retirement-plan savings when you need the money the most and are the most vulnerable because you are not working.

- At the time of this writing, it has a guaranteed 4+% tax-deferred rate of return and a guaranteed locked-in 5% loan rate.

- Many big-name advisers recommend you buy term insurance and invest the difference. However, many individuals don't invest the difference but spend it. The Personal Bank has built-in self-discipline, ensuring you do have money in retirement.

- You may also have access to the life-insurance benefits before you pass away should you have a terminal illness, critical illness, or chronic illness, making the policy like a long-term care policy.

- You never have to worry about the volatility of the stock market.

- You have guaranteed insurability for your life, and, when you die, the death benefit goes 100% income tax-free to your heirs. Without proper planning, as much as 75 percent of your estate could be lost to legal fees, estate-administration costs, and estate taxes.

Cash-value life insurance provides a tax-free death benefit that bypasses probate altogether. There is no better asset to die with than life insurance.

- Cash-value life insurance remains one of the last places where you can draw money and not have it count against this social security tax.

- You have access to the cash value in the policy without penalties or restrictions.

- You reverse the flow of interest you are paying to the bank back to paying the interest to yourself.

- You pay no income or capital-gains taxes on policy loans and most withdrawals.

- It does not require any dramatic lifestyle changes and provides money for purchases and retirement needs.

- The interest and dividends are paid on all the money you have put into the policy, even if you have borrowed money from the policy to spend.

- The owner and the insured do not have to be the same person. The wife can be the owner of the policy, and the insured could be her husband or child. If sole owner, she has complete control of the cash value in the policy and not the insured. If health and age do not allow you to get the insurance you need, you own the insurance policy on the life of another person.

- The death benefit is a great side benefit to these policies. It can be critical to leave a legacy and to care for your family and can be a jump-start of future wealth for your family. As the cash value grows, your death benefit also grows. The older you get, the more money is passed on to your family. Though nothing is certain except death and taxes, you can at least minimize your taxes. Under current tax law, your death benefit (less any outstanding loans) passes income tax-free to your loved ones, favorite charities, or other beneficiaries.

- Unlike 401(k)s or other government-controlled retirement plans, there are no government minimum or maximum contributions to a cash-value life insurance policy as long as you abide by the IRS MEC rules. You can contribute as much or as little as you want. The only limit is how much insurance the insurance company is willing to offer.

- You have unrestricted liquidity, control, and use of your money for any reason.

- Reduces the chance you will do stupid things with your money.

- There is great flexibility in the policy. Many people mistakenly think that you must pay premiums each year into a whole-life policy to keep it active. This is just not true. You can front-load your policy with high premium payments for 2 to 4 years, and then the policy is paid in full. You can also reduce the amount you pay into the policy each year if you have restricted cash flow—just pay the basic premium. When you have more money, put more in. There is great flexibility with the companies I have mentioned, and a good insurance agent can help you with your questions.

- In many states, these assets are protected from creditors, judgments, and lawsuits.

- You can build your wealth tax free and access your wealth tax free (provided an MEC does not occur or a lapse or surrender with a gain, as this would result in a taxable event).

- It helps you pay off debt, invest, and save at the same time. Pay off your cars, home, student loans, and credit cards while simultaneously building retirement wealth using the same dollars.

PERSONAL BANK EXAMPLE

Here is an example of a high-cash-value, whole-life policy for a 40-year-old male non-smoker with annual outlay of $10,000. Note that the cash value always continues to grow as well as the death benefit. At age 65, his cash value has grown to $445,154, with a death benefit of $882,514. If he started at age 30 and put in $30,000 for 25 years, his cash value would be more than $2,166,549 and have a death benefit of considerably more than $3 million at age 65. If we use the example family in this book, who after paying off their debt, will have more than $30,000 annually to put toward their Personal Bank. By age 65, they would have more than $1,333,462 in cash value and a death benefit of more than $2.6 million. Remember, they always have available that additional $30,000 each year in their cash value to buy cars, take vacations, and send their children to college, while the cash value in their policy is always growing. When you become debt free, you could easily put much more into your Personal Bank, such as $20,000, $50,000, $100,000, or even $300,000 a year, depending on your income. You will never worry about what the stock market is doing, knowing that your financial and retirement needs have been guaranteed and that you will be leaving a legacy for your family. Note that there is a guaranteed portion which you can always count on, as well as the current assumption based on recent dividends which you most likely would receive.

It is important to understand that there is a difference between dividend rate and the real annual net return in these high-cash-value, whole-life policies. The actual net rate of return is usually

40-YEAR-OLD MALE. $10,000/YR – 25 YEARS

Yr	Age	Age/Funding Annual Outlay	Cum. Outlay	GUARANTEED Cash Value	Death Benefit	CURRENT ASSUMPTIONS Cash Value	Death Benefit
1	41	$10,000	$10,000	$8,463	$277,680	$8,609	$277,680
2	42	$10,000	$20,000	$16,970	$304,425	$17,653	$304,903
3	43	$10,000	$30,000	$26,449	$330,269	$27,929	$331,688
4	44	$10,000	$40,000	$36,350	$355,250	$38,866	$358,072
5	45	$10,000	$50,000	$46,533	$379,402	$50,360	$384,093
6	46	$10,000	$60,000	$56,999	$402,760	$62,418	$409,804
7	47	$10,000	$70,000	$67,758	$425,357	$75,063	$435,241
8	48	$10,000	$80,000	$78,814	$447,226	$88,325	$460,441
9	49	$10,000	$90,000	$90,216	$468,393	$102,235	$485,444
10	50	$10,000	$100,000	$101,966	$488,883	$116,822	$510,203
11	51	$10,000	$110,000	$114,064	$508,718	$132,137	$534,736
12	52	$10,000	$120,000	$126,490	$527,921	$148,190	$559,131
13	53	$10,000	$130,000	$139,218	$546,515	$165,026	$583,397
14	54	$10,000	$140,000	$152,234	$564,526	$182,668	$607,610
15	55	$10,000	$150,000	$165,503	$581,977	$201,164	$631,795
16	56	$10,000	$160,000	$178,896	$598,895	$220,559	$656,056

40-YEAR-OLD MALE. $10,000/YR – 25 YEARS

Yr	Age	Age/Funding Annual Outlay	Cum. Outlay	GUARANTEED Cash Value	GUARANTEED Death Benefit	CURRENT ASSUMPTIONS Cash Value	CURRENT ASSUMPTIONS Death Benefit
17	57	$10,000	$170,000	$192,499	$615,304	$240,979	$680,456
18	58	$10,000	$180,000	$206,291	$631,227	$262,450	$705,000
19	59	$10,000	$190,000	$220,346	$646,686	$285,021	$729,699
20	60	$10,000	$200,000	$234,632	$661,700	$308,752	$754,461
21	61	$10,000	$210,000	$249,103	$676,284	$333,614	$779,344
22	62	$10,000	$220,000	$263,673	$690,457	$359,637	$804,482
23	63	$10,000	$230,000	$278,250	$704,238	$386,889	$829,973
24	64	$10,000	$240,000	$292,769	$717,647	$415,385	$855,976
25	65	$10,000	$250,000	$307,217	$730,702	$445,154	$882,514
26	66	$0		$315,137	$563,277	$467,580	$835,756
30	70	$0		$347,440	$563,277	$568,407	$921,512
35	75	$0		$388,537	$563,277	$722,183	$1,046,976
40	80	$0		$427,978	$563,277	$909,880	$1,197,526
45	85	$0		$462,366	$563,277	$1,132,824	$1,380,062
50	90	$0		$489,882	$563,277	$1,386,201	$1,593,884

1% to 2% lower than the company's announced dividend rate, because net rate is calculated after the company's insurance expenses and mortality charges. If the dividend rate is 6%, then you can expect a tax-free net internal rate of return (IRR) between 4% and 5% with current assumptions. The 1% to 2% may vary, depending on the age and health of the insured. Also, the actual guaranteed net return will also be 1% to 2% lower resulting in a tax-free net internal rate of return of 1% to 3%. The guaranteed rates are lower because they cannot guarantee dividends even though they have been paid every year for more than 150 years by Guardian and Mass Mutual insurance companies. All illustrations presented in this chapter are based on the current dividend scale. In the illustration below, you will see the guaranteed and current assumed annual tax-deferred returns for a 40-year-old male whose annual outlay each year is $10,000 for 25 years.

40-YEAR-OLD MALE — $10,000/YR — 25 YEARS POLICY

	Age/Funding			GUARANTEED		CURRENT ASSUMPTIONS		NET (IRR) Returns	Average Returns
Yr	Age	Annual Outlay	Cum. Outlay	Cash Value	Death Benefit	Cash Value	Death Benefit		
1	41	$10,000	$10,000	$8,463	$277,680	$8,609	$277,680	-13.91%	-13.91%
2	42	$10,000	$20,000	$16,970	$304,425	$17,653	$304,903	-5.14%	-8.04%
3	43	$10,000	$30,000	$26,449	$330,269	$27,929	$331,688	1.00%	-3.54%
4	44	$10,000	$40,000	$36,350	$355,250	$38,866	$358,072	2.47%	-1.15%
5	45	$10,000	$50,000	$46,533	$379,402	$50,360	$384,093	3.06%	0.24%
6	46	$10,000	$60,000	$56,999	$402,760	$62,418	$409,804	3.41%	1.13%
7	47	$10,000	$70,000	$67,758	$425,357	$75,063	$435,241	3.65%	1.75%
8	48	$10,000	$80,000	$78,814	$447,226	$88,325	$460,441	3.84%	2.20%
9	49	$10,000	$90,000	$90,216	$468,393	$102,235	$485,444	3.98%	2.54%
10	50	$10,000	$100,000	$101,966	$488,883	$116,822	$510,203	4.09%	2.81%
11	51	$10,000	$110,000	$114,064	$508,718	$132,137	$534,736	4.19%	3.03%
12	52	$10,000	$120,000	$126,490	$527,921	$148,190	$559,131	4.26%	3.21%
13	53	$10,000	$130,000	$139,218	$546,515	$165,026	$583,397	4.32%	3.35%
14	54	$10,000	$140,000	$152,234	$564,526	$182,668	$607,610	4.37%	3.48%
15	55	$10,000	$150,000	$165,503	$581,977	$201,164	$631,795	4.41%	3.59%
16	56	$10,000	$160,000	$178,896	$598,895	$220,559	$656,056	4.45%	3.68%

40-YEAR-OLD MALE — $10,000/YR — 25 YEARS POLICY

Age/Funding				GUARANTEED		CURRENT ASSUMPTIONS			
Yr	Age	Annual Outlay	Cum. Outlay	Cash Value	Death Benefit	Cash Value	Death Benefit	NET (IRR) Returns	Average Returns
17	57	$10,000	$170,000	$192,499	$615,304	$240,979	$680,456	4.52%	3.76%
18	58	$10,000	$180,000	$206,291	$631,227	$262,450	$705,000	4.57%	3.84%
19	59	$10,000	$190,000	$220,346	$646,686	$285,021	$729,699	4.61%	3.91%
20	60	$10,000	$200,000	$234,632	$661,700	$308,752	$754,461	4.65%	3.97%
21	61	$10,000	$210,000	$249,103	$676,284	$333,614	$779,344	4.66%	4.03%
22	62	$10,000	$220,000	$263,673	$690,457	$359,637	$804,482	4.66%	4.08%
23	63	$10,000	$230,000	$278,250	$704,238	$386,889	$829,973	4.67%	4.12%
24	64	$10,000	$240,000	$292,769	$717,647	$415,385	$855,976	4.66%	4.16%
25	65	$10,000	$250,000	$307,217	$730,702	$445,154	$882,514	4.65%	4.19%
26	66	$0		$315,137	$563,277	$467,580	$835,756	5.04%	4.24%
30	70	$0		$347,440	$563,277	$568,407	$921,512	5.00%	4.33%
35	75	$0		$388,537	$563,277	$722,183	$1,046,976	4.91%	4.46%
40	80	$0		$427,978	$563,277	$909,880	$1,197,526	4.73%	4.52%
45	85	$0		$462,366	$563,277	$1,132,824	$1,380,062	4.48%	4.53%
50	90	$0		$489,882	$563,277	$1,386,201	$1,593,884	4.12%	4.50%

Most Americans are shocked when they start accessing their retirement income from their 401(k) plan and finally understand the effect of 30% to 40% taxes on their returns. Also, according to *Forbes,* the average investor in a blend of equities and fixed-income mutual funds has earned only a 2.6% or less net annualized rate of return. Below is a modified chart showing the equivalent tax-free returns of an individual in a 35% tax bracket. Most investors also forget about the 2% fee paid their financial adviser and mutual-fund company. A whole-life policy does not have these fees and should be added to the true net return. The last column demonstrates the return when the insured dies unexpectedly and the death benefit is passed on tax-free to their family. Remember that 401(k)s and other retirement plans do not have a death benefit.

40-YEAR-OLD MALE — $10,000/YR — 25 YEARS POLICY

	Age/Funding					CURRENT ASSUMPTIONS			
Yr	Age	Annual Outlay	Cum. Outlay	Cash Value	Death Benefit	Net (IRR) Returns	Equivalent 35% tax return	With 2% advisory fees	Percent if death occurs
1	41	$10,000	$10,000	$8,609	$277,680	-13.91%			
2	42	$10,000	$20,000	$17,653	$304,903	-5.14%			
3	43	$10,000	$30,000	$27,929	$331,688	1.00%	1.53%	3.53%	1099.48%
4	44	$10,000	$40,000	$38,866	$358,072	2.47%	3.80%	5.80%	844.07%
5	45	$10,000	$50,000	$50,360	$384,093	3.06%	4.70%	6.70%	686.01%
6	46	$10,000	$60,000	$62,418	$409,804	3.41%	5.25%	7.25%	578.93%
7	47	$10,000	$70,000	$75,063	$435,241	3.65%	5.62%	7.62%	501.01%
8	48	$10,000	$80,000	$88,325	$460,441	3.84%	5.90%	7.90%	441.30%
9	49	$10,000	$90,000	$102,235	$485,444	3.98%	6.12%	8.12%	393.71%
10	50	$10,000	$100,000	$116,822	$510,203	4.09%	6.29%	8.29%	354.58%
11	51	$10,000	$110,000	$132,137	$534,736	4.19%	6.45%	8.45%	321.64%
12	52	$10,000	$120,000	$148,190	$559,131	4.26%	6.55%	8.55%	293.38%
13	53	$10,000	$130,000	$165,026	$583,397	4.32%	6.65%	8.65%	268.79%
14	54	$10,000	$140,000	$182,668	$607,610	4.37%	6.72%	8.72%	247.15%
15	55	$10,000	$150,000	$201,164	$631,795	4.41%	6.78%	8.78%	227.92%
16	56	$10,000	$160,000	$220,559	$656,056	4.45%	6.84%	8.84%	210.69%

40-YEAR-OLD MALE — $10,000/YR — 25 YEARS POLICY

	Age/Funding					CURRENT ASSUMPTIONS			
Yr	Age	Annual Outlay	Cum. Outlay	Cash Value	Death Benefit	Net (IRR) Returns	Equivalent 35% tax return	With 2% advisory fees	Percent if death occurs
17	57	$10,000	$170,000	$240,979	$680,456	4.52%	6.95%	8.95%	195.13%
18	58	$10,000	$180,000	$262,450	$705,000	4.57%	7.03%	9.03%	180.90%
19	59	$10,000	$190,000	$285,021	$729,699	4.61%	7.10%	9.10%	167.83%
20	60	$10,000	$200,000	$308,752	$754,461	4.65%	7.16%	9.16%	155.73%
21	61	$10,000	$210,000	$333,614	$779,344	4.66%	7.17%	9.17%	144.50%
22	62	$10,000	$220,000	$359,637	$804,482	4.66%	7.17%	9.17%	134.12%
23	63	$10,000	$230,000	$386,889	$829,973	4.67%	7.18%	9.18%	124.54%
24	64	$10,000	$240,000	$415,385	$855,976	4.66%	7.17%	9.17%	115.67%
25	65	$10,000	$250,000	$445,154	$882,514	4.65%	7.15%	9.15%	107.46%
26	66	$0		$467,580	$835,756	5.04%	7.75%	9.75%	87.75%
30	70	$0		$568,407	$921,512	5.00%	7.70%	9.70%	97.08%
35	75	$0		$722,183	$1,046,976	4.91%	7.55%	9.55%	84.19%
40	80	$0		$909,880	$1,197,526	4.73%	7.28%	9.28%	65.82%
45	85	$0		$1,132,824	$1,380,062	4.48%	6.89%	8.89%	51.68%
50	90	$0		$1,386,201	$1,593,884	4.12%	6.34%	8.34%	40.70%

PERSONAL BANK SCENARIOS

Below are two condensed charts of the 40-year-old male non-smoker comparing putting in $10,000 and $100,000 each year into their Personal Bank. Note that the $100,000 policy is 10 times that of the $10,000 policy. (See chart below).

40-YEAR-OLD MALE — 25 YEARS POLICY					
Yr	Age	Annual Outlay	Cum. Outlay	Cash Value	Death Benefit
1	41	$10,000	$10,000	$8,609	$277,680
5	45	$10,000	$50,000	$50,360	$384,093
10	50	$10,000	$100,000	$116,822	$510,203
15	55	$10,000	$150,000	$201,164	$631,795
20	60	$10,000	$200,000	$308,752	$754,461
25	65	$10,000	$250,000	$445,154	$882,514
26	66	0	$250,000	$467,580	$835,756
30	70	0	$250,000	$568,407	$921,512
35	75	0	$250,000	$722,183	$1,046,976
40	80	0	$250,000	$909,880	$1,197,526
45	85	0	$250,000	$1,132,824	$1,380,062
50	90	0	$250,000	$1,386,201	$1,593,884

40-YEAR-OLD MALE — 25 YEARS POLICY					
Yr	Age	Annual Outlay	Cum. Outlay	Cash Value	Death Benefit
1	41	$100,000	$100,000	$86,094	$2,776,803
5	45	$100,000	$500,000	$503,602	$3,840,932
10	50	$100,000	$1,000,000	$1,168,215	$5,201,025
15	55	$100,000	$1,500,000	$2,011,640	$6,317,948
20	60	$100,000	$2,000,000	$3,087,520	$7,544,614
25	65	$100,000	$2,500,000	$4,451,536	$8,825,143
26	66	0	$2,500,000	$4,675,805	$8,357,561
30	70	0	$2,500,000	$5,684,068	$9,215,116
35	75	0	$2,500,000	$7,221,830	$10,469,758
40	80	0	$2,500,000	$9,098,805	$11,975,263
45	85	0	$2,500,000	$11,328,238	$13,800,619
50	90	0	$2,500,000	$13,862,005	$15,938,836

If you wanted to put $30,000 each year into your policy, you would simply multiply the cash value and death benefit in the $10,000 policy by three to get your ballpark returns. At age 65, the person who put in $10,000 a year will have $445,154 in cash value and $882,514 in death benefits. And if he was able to put in $100,000 each year, he would have had $4,451,536 in cash value and $8,825,143 in death benefits. When individuals become debt free, many have an extra $100,000, $200,000, or even $300,000 per year that they could put in this tax-deferred, tax-free Personal Bank to fund their life. $300,000 invested each year would give the individual a cash value at age 65 of $13,354,608 and a permanent death benefit of $26,475,429.

Yr	Age	Annual Outlay	Cum. Outlay	Cash Value	Death Benefit
1	41	$300,000	$300,000	$258,281	$8,330,408
5	45	$300,000	$1,500,000	$1,510,805	$11,522,797
10	50	$300,000	$3,000,000	$3,504,645	$15,306,076
15	55	$300,000	$4,500,000	$6,034,919	$18,953,845
20	60	$300,000	$6,000,000	$9,262,561	$22,633,843
25	65	$300,000	$7,500,000	$13,354,608	$26,475,429
26	66	0	$7,500,000	$14,207,414	$25,072,682
30	70	0	$7,500,000	$17,052,203	$27,645,347
35	75	0	$7,500,000	$21,665,489	$31,409,275
40	80	0	$7,500,000	$27,296,415	$35,925,789
45	85	0	$7,500,000	$33,984,714	$41,401,857
50	90	0	$7,500,000	$41,586,016	$47,816,507

40-YEAR-OLD MALE — 25 YEARS POLICY

It is never too late to buy a whole-life insurance policy to create your own Personal Bank. Here is an example of a 50-year-old who could put in $10,000 for 15 years.

50-YEAR-OLD Male — 15 YEAR POLICY				
Year	Age	Annual Outlay	Net Cash	Death Benefit
1	51	$10,000	$8,420	$203,826
2	52	$10,000	$17,258	$227,285
3	53	$10,000	$27,347	$250,388
4	54	$10,000	$37,966	$273,144
5	55	$10,000	$49,102	$295,575
6	56	$10,000	$60,794	$317,694
7	57	$10,000	$73,042	$339,533
8	58	$10,000	$85,864	$361,131
9	59	$10,000	$99,282	$382,516
10	60	$10,000	$113,309	$403,701
11	61	$10,000	$128,011	$424,715
12	62	$10,000	$143,402	$445,665
13	63	$10,000	$159,494	$466,579
14	64	$10,000	$175,305	$487,475
15	65	$10,000	$193,844	$508,383
16	66	$0	$202,605	$394,657
20	70	$0	$244,463	$426,095
25	75	$0	$309,650	$475,054
30	80	$0	$388,222	$532,914
35	85	$0	$480,432	$599,499
40	90	$0	$582,783	$677,072
45	95	$0	$688,524	$759,843
50	100	$0	$835,209	$835,209

At age 59½ you can access your retirement plans without a penalty. Many of those who can see the true benefits of a high-cash-value, whole-life insurance policy are taking money out of their retirement plans, paying the tax, and putting that money into their own safe Personal Bank. It is always much more effective to spread the lump-sum payments over a five-year period instead of just one year. Here are some examples.

60- & 65-YEAR OLD Male. Minimum Premium. $100,000 MEC Limit

60-Year-Old Male

Yr	Age	Annual Outlay	Cumulative Outlay	Cash Value	Death Benefit
1	60	$100,000	$100,000	$88,058	$1,430,000
2	61	$100,000	$200,000	$189,410	$1,430,000
3	62	$100,000	$300,000	$293,398	$1,430,000
4	63	$100,000	$400,000	$405,400	$1,430,000
5	64	$100,000	$500,000	$523,477	$1,430,000
6	65	$0		$548,062	$1,430,000
7	66	$0		$573,585	$1,430,000
8	67	$0		$601,769	$1,122,501
9	68	$0		$631,266	$1,139,626
10	69	$0		$662,136	$1,157,593
11	70	$0		$693,761	$1,176,488
12	71	$0		$726,788	$1,196,333
13	72	$0		$761,149	$1,217,244

65-Year-Old Male

Yr	Age	Annual Outlay	Cumulative Outlay	Cash Value	Death Benefit
1	65	$100,000	$100,000	$87,500	$1,210,000
2	66	$100,000	$200,000	$188,209	$1,210,000
3	67	$100,000	$300,000	$291,453	$1,210,000
4	68	$100,000	$400,000	$402,600	$1,210,000
5	69	$100,000	$500,000	$519,788	$1,210,000
6	70	$0		$543,493	$1,210,000
7	71	$0		$568,074	$1,210,000
8	72	$0		$594,992	$974,044
9	73	$0		$622,992	$988,488
10	74	$0		$652,137	$1,003,883
11	75	$0		$681,461	$1,020,314
12	76	$0		$711,935	$1,037,794
13	77	$0		$743,564	$1,056,287

60- & 65-YEAR OLD Male. Minimum Premium. $100,000 MEC Limit

60-Year-Old Male

Yr	Age	Annual Outlay	Cumulative Outlay	Cash Value	Death Benefit
14	73	$0		$796,946	$1,239,149
15	74	$0		$834,256	$1,262,277
16	75	$0		$873,148	$1,286,743
17	76	$0		$913,639	$1,312,567
18	77	$0		$955,744	$1,339,711
19	78	$0		$999,469	$1,368,059
20	79	$0		$1,044,765	$1,397,533
21	80	$0		$1,091,933	$1,428,084
22	81	$0		$1,140,802	$1,459,786
23	82	$0		$1,191,510	$1,492,791
24	83	$0		$1,244,134	$1,527,212
25	84	$0		$1,298,620	$1,563,483

65-Year-Old Male

Yr	Age	Annual Outlay	Cumulative Outlay	Cash Value	Death Benefit
14	78	$0		$776,347	$1,075,693
15	79	$0		$810,243	$1,095,945
16	80	$0		$845,311	$1,116,997
17	81	$0		$881,596	$1,138,946
18	82	$0		$919,200	$1,161,907
19	83	$0		$958,180	$1,185,968
20	84	$0		$998,480	$1,211,475
21	85	$0		$1,040,494	$1,238,458
22	86	$0		$1,083,484	$1,266,970
23	87	$0		$1,127,509	$1,296,779
24	88	$0		$1,172,421	$1,328,083
25	89	$0		$1,218,223	$1,360,854

One of the main advantages of a Personal Bank is to have tax-free income during retirement. Below is a 45-year-old who has put $100,000 a year in for 20 years and at age 65 can take out $150,000 per year tax-free up to age 95. This is done through a loan process from the insurance company's general fund, making the income tax free. This $150,000 is like a withdrawal from an IRA of $225,000 that is taxable.

45-YEAR-OLD Male $100,000/yr for 20 Years

Growth

Yr	Age	Annual Outlay	Cash Value	Death Benefit
1	45	$100,000	$85,040	$6,400,000
2	46	$100,000	$175,485	$6,400,000
3	47	$100,000	$275,594	$6,400,000
4	48	$100,000	$384,400	$6,400,000
5	49	$100,000	$498,883	$6,400,000
6	50	$100,000	$619,152	$6,400,000
7	51	$100,000	$745,399	$6,400,000
8	52	$100,000	$877,842	$6,400,000
9	53	$100,000	$1,016,948	$6,400,000
10	54	$100,000	$1,162,910	$6,400,000
11	55	$100,000	$1,316,052	$6,400,000
12	56	$100,000	$1,476,945	$6,400,000
13	57	$100,000	$1,645,916	$6,400,000
14	58	$100,000	$1,823,640	$6,400,000
15	59	$100,000	$2,010,535	$6,400,000
16	60	$100,000	$2,206,918	$6,400,000
17	61	$100,000	$2,413,263	$6,400,000
18	62	$100,000	$2,630,104	$6,400,000

Income

Yr	Age	Annual Outlay	Annual Income	Cash Value	Death Benefit
1	45	$100,000	$0	$85,040	$6,400,000
2	46	$100,000	$0	$175,485	$6,400,000
3	47	$100,000	$0	$275,594	$6,400,000
4	48	$100,000	$0	$384,400	$6,400,000
5	49	$100,000	$0	$498,883	$6,400,000
6	50	$100,000	$0	$619,152	$6,400,000
7	51	$100,000	$0	$745,399	$6,400,000
8	52	$100,000	$0	$877,842	$6,400,000
9	53	$100,000	$0	$1,016,948	$6,400,000
10	54	$100,000	$0	$1,162,910	$6,400,000
11	55	$100,000	$0	$1,316,052	$6,400,000
12	56	$100,000	$0	$1,476,945	$6,400,000
13	57	$100,000	$0	$1,645,916	$6,400,000
14	58	$100,000	$0	$1,823,640	$6,400,000
15	59	$100,000	$0	$2,010,535	$6,400,000
16	60	$100,000	$0	$2,206,918	$6,400,000
17	61	$100,000	$0	$2,413,263	$6,400,000
18	62	$100,000	$0	$2,630,104	$6,400,000

45-YEAR-OLD Male $100,000/yr for 20 Years

	Growth					Income				
Yr	Age	Annual Outlay	Cash Value	Death Benefit	Yr	Age	Annual Outlay	Annual Income	Cash Value	Death Benefit
19	63	$100,000	$2,858,008	$6,400,000	19	63	$100,000	$0	$2,858,008	$6,400,000
20	64	$100,000	$3,097,650	$6,400,000	20	64	$100,000	$0	$3,097,650	$6,400,000
21	65	$0	$3,248,239	$6,127,342	21	65		-150,000	$3,088,524	$5,826,439
22	66	$0	$3,405,483	$6,240,296	22	66		-150,000	$3,078,326	$5,642,836
23	67	$0	$3,569,757	$6,356,841	23	67		-150,000	$3,067,110	$5,465,173
24	68	$0	$3,741,327	$6,477,109	24	68		-150,000	$3,054,817	$5,293,172
25	69	$0	$3,920,732	$6,601,239	25	69		-150,000	$3,041,591	$5,126,564
26	70	$0	$4,107,847	$6,729,713	26	70		-150,000	$3,027,043	$4,965,357
27	71	$0	$4,303,039	$6,862,663	27	71		-150,000	$3,011,172	$4,809,224
28	72	$0	$4,505,792	$7,000,714	28	72		-150,000	$2,993,373	$4,658,193
29	73	$0	$4,716,533	$7,143,522	29	73		-150,000	$2,973,711	$4,511,582
30	74	$0	$4,935,658	$7,292,073	30	74		-150,000	$2,952,213	$4,369,596
31	75	$0	$5,163,372	$7,447,038	31	75		-150,000	$2,928,775	$4,232,175
32	76	$0	$5,399,955	$7,608,553	32	76		-150,000	$2,903,335	$4,098,923
33	77	$0	$5,645,377	$7,776,420	33	77		-150,000	$2,875,667	$3,969,295
34	78	$0	$5,899,496	$7,950,120	34	78		-150,000	$2,845,475	$3,882,035
35	79	$0	$6,162,208	$8,129,020	35	79		-150,000	$2,808,835	$3,808,867
36	80	$0	$6,433,795	$8,313,039	36	80		-150,000	$2,766,814	$3,727,540

45-YEAR-OLD Male $100,000/yr for 20 Years

		Growth					Income			
Yr	Age	Annual Outlay	Cash Value	Death Benefit	Yr	Age	Annual Outlay	Annual Income	Cash Value	Death Benefit
37	81	$0	$6,714,566	$8,502,879	37	81	$0	-150,000	$2,719,038	$3,638,412
38	82	$0	$7,005,204	$8,699,279	38	82	$0	-150,000	$2,665,298	$3,541,472
39	83	$0	$7,305,907	$8,902,871	39	83	$0	-150,000	$2,605,111	$3,436,634
40	84	$0	$7,616,469	$9,116,208	40	84	$0	-150,000	$2,537,728	$3,324,726
41	85	$0	$7,936,185	$9,339,554	41	85	$0	-150,000	$2,462,213	$3,205,343
42	86	$0	$8,262,636	$9,573,471	42	86	$0	-150,000	$2,376,691	$3,078,293
43	87	$0	$8,596,182	$9,816,409	43	87	$0	-150,000	$2,280,679	$2,942,201
44	88	$0	$8,935,119	$10,070,214	44	88	$0	-150,000	$2,172,671	$2,797,373
45	89	$0	$9,279,005	$10,334,662	45	89	$0	-150,000	$2,051,725	$2,643,051
46	90	$0	$9,627,129	$10,609,714	46	90	$0	-150,000	$1,916,800	$2,478,488
47	91	$0	$9,978,580	$10,895,217	47	91	$0	-150,000	$1,766,710	$2,302,893
48	92	$0	$10,332,650	$11,189,728	48	92	$0	-150,000	$1,600,419	$2,114,801
49	93	$0	$10,688,182	$11,491,381	49	93	$0	-150,000	$1,416,579	$1,912,611
50	94	$0	$11,046,706	$11,797,866	50	94	$0	-150,000	$1,215,182	$1,694,418

Using the Personal Bank to create a family legacy

The foundation of a Personal Bank is a whole-life insurance policy that will be in effect during the whole life of the individual who is covered by the policy. Upon that person's death (even at an early age), the family will receive an income tax-free benefit or legacy. This could be a significant amount of money that provides safety and security for their family. This is in addition to any other assets of the individual.

Another type of legacy can be created by parents or grandparents through funding individual Personal Banks for their children or grandchildren. The individual policy will be on the child, but the parent will be the owner and beneficiary of the policy and cash value in the policy. The cash value will grow tax-deferred every year and be available for the parent as a bank account to support the child if they want to buy a car, go to college, get married, buy a house, or open a business. The ownership of the policy can be transferred to the child when they are mature enough to handle the cash value of the policy. Below is an example of a $10,000 policy on a three-year-old. This is a much better way to save for a college education compared to a 529 plan that has many governmental restrictions, as previously covered above. As the child pays back these tax-free loans from the policy, the money continues to grow as if they'd never taken out a loan at all. At age 18, the child will have $221,873 available for their education. At age 26, the child will have $415,888 to buy a home, start a family, or start a business. The child will never have to use a regular bank. And at age 62, the child will have $2,846,101 available tax-free for their retirement.

Yr	Age	Annual Outlay	Cash Value	Death Benefit
1	3	$10,000	$8,509	$1,009,743
2	4	$10,000	$17,597	$1,117,646
3	5	$10,000	$27,912	$1,223,286
4	6	$10,000	$38,785	$1,326,599
5	7	$10,000	$50,260	$1,427,908
6	8	$10,000	$62,345	$1,527,323
7	9	$10,000	$75,061	$1,624,872
8	10	$10,000	$88,452	$1,720,631
9	11	$10,000	$102,555	$1,814,754
10	12	$10,000	$117,389	$1,907,316
11	13	$10,000	$132,988	$1,998,627
12	14	$10,000	$149,338	$2,089,129
13	15	$10,000	$166,450	$2,178,749
14	16	$10,000	$184,244	$2,267,631
15	17	$10,000	$202,710	$2,355,928
16	18	$10,000	$221,873	$2,443,650
17	19	$10,000	$241,927	$2,530,783
18	20	$10,000	$263,044	$2,616,993
19	21	$10,000	$285,273	$2,702,968
20	22	$10,000	$308,753	$2,788,455
21	23	$10,000	$333,503	$2,873,330
22	24	$10,000	$359,564	$2,958,022
23	25	$10,000	$387,019	$3,042,234
24	26	$10,000	$415,888	$3,126,135
25	27	$10,000	$446,327	$3,209,588
26	28	$10,000	$478,406	$3,293,324
27	29	$10,000	$512,371	$3,377,517
28	30	$10,000	$548,154	$3,461,873
29	31	$10,000	$585,899	$3,545,690
30	32	$10,000	$625,641	$3,629,198

Yr	Age	Annual Outlay	Cash Value	Death Benefit
31	33	$0	$657,665	$3,622,983
32	34	$0	$691,386	$3,616,900
33	35	$0	$726,917	$3,610,918
34	36	$0	$764,349	$3,605,381
35	37	$0	$803,704	$3,600,292
36	38	$0	$845,049	$3,613,330
37	39	$0	$888,534	$3,666,220
38	40	$0	$934,265	$3,720,458
39	41	$0	$982,321	$3,776,146
40	42	$0	$1,032,808	$3,833,143
41	43	$0	$1,085,968	$3,891,684
42	44	$0	$1,141,987	$3,952,471
43	45	$0	$1,200,974	$4,015,653
44	46	$0	$1,263,186	$4,081,713
45	47	$0	$1,328,704	$4,150,965
46	48	$0	$1,397,801	$4,222,936
47	49	$0	$1,470,651	$4,297,917
48	50	$0	$1,547,373	$4,374,909
49	51	$0	$1,628,251	$4,453,860
50	52	$0	$1,713,303	$4,535,149
51	53	$0	$1,802,750	$4,618,877
52	54	$0	$1,896,776	$4,705,573
53	55	$0	$1,995,602	$4,795,481
54	56	$0	$2,099,471	$4,889,176
55	57	$0	$2,208,849	$4,987,341
56	58	$0	$2,323,884	$5,090,206
57	59	$0	$2,444,909	$5,197,899
58	60	$0	$2,572,132	$5,309,244
59	61	$0	$2,705,858	$5,424,514
60	62	$0	$2,846,101	$5,544,287

Below will be another example of older parents transferring wealth to their children through a Personal Bank. In this example, the parents purchase a whole-life policy on their 31-year-old son-in-law for $30,000 a year for 25 years, making the daughter beneficiary and owner of the policy. She will be the beneficiary of the policy and have complete control of the money in the policy unless designated differently by the parents. This cash value in the policy can be used by this couple to pay down debt, while, over time, returning the borrowed money back into cash value. After 10 years the children are debt-free and have $349,346 in their own Personal Bank. This Personal Bank can be used over the years for purchases for which they would normally have to borrow money from a regular bank to cover. At age 65, they will have $2,175,476 for their tax-free retirement; if it is not used, this sum will continue to grow every year thereafter. This is true legacy.

30-YEAR-OLD Male — 25-YEAR POLICY

Year	Age	Annual Outlay	Net Cash	Death Benefit	Year	Age	Annual Outlay	Net Cash	Death Benefit
1	31	$30,000	$26,247	$1,193,475	19	49	$30,000	$853,739	$3,535,655
2	32	$30,000	$53,817	$1,337,527	20	50	$30,000	$924,802	$3,654,811
3	33	$30,000	$84,366	$1,479,122	21	51	$30,000	$999,142	$3,772,897
4	34	$30,000	$116,892	$1,618,387	22	52	$30,000	$1,076,972	$3,889,933
5	35	$30,000	$151,067	$1,755,520	23	53	$30,000	$1,158,465	$4,006,005
6	36	$30,000	$186,949	$1,890,706	24	54	$30,000	$1,243,750	$4,121,393
7	37	$30,000	$224,652	$2,024,046	25	55	$30,000	$1,332,949	$4,236,120
8	38	$30,000	$264,229	$2,156,023	26	56	$0	$1,399,786	$3,704,704
9	39	$30,000	$305,802	$2,286,510	30	60	$0	$1,703,267	$3,696,948
10	40	$30,000	$349,346	$2,415,857	35	65	$0	$2,176,476	$4,363,337
11	41	$30,000	$395,109	$2,543,914	40	70	$0	$2,772,973	$4,833,237
12	42	$30,000	$443,174	$2,671,214	45	75	$0	$3,508,744	$5,382,995
13	43	$30,000	$493,646	$2,797,844	50	80	$0	$4,391,527	$6,028,260
14	44	$30,000	$546,611	$2,923,698	55	85	$0	$5,420,030	$6,763,286
15	45	$30,000	$602,173	$3,048,384	60	90	$0	$6,555,632	$7,616,274
16	46	$30,000	$660,482	$3,171,908	65	95	$0	$7,764,557	$8,568,828
17	47	$30,000	$721,739	$3,294,279	70	100	$0	$9,432,499	$9,432,499
18	48	$30,000	$786,114	$3,415,502					

How safe are these companies? Many of the large companies such as Guardian and Mass Mutual have been around for more than 160 years and have paid dividends every year. These companies are mutual insurance companies, which, essentially, are owned by its policy owners, not stockholders. This lets them focus on long-term interests of policyholders instead of short-term demands on Wall Street. By law they have to have at least 100% liquid cash available to pay off a death benefit. For every dollar of insurance in force, they have to have one dollar +3 cents in liquid cash in reserves. To check out the companies' assets and investments, go to their vital-signs report. More than 50% of their investments are in bonds. They also invest in high-end, income-producing commercial real estate and other businesses. Life-insurance companies are audited regularly by the insurance commissioners of the states they do business in to make sure they maintain enough reserves to be able to pay all claims and are financially sound. If a company fails to maintain proper reserves or gets into financial difficulty, the state insurance commissioner's office will step in, take over the company, and run it in the interest of the policyholders. Usually, a failed insurance business is taken over by another company. They are also audited and regulated by several different independent rating services. Each state has an insurance guaranty fund that insures the cash value and death benefit of all policies up to a certain limit.

Other important aspects about whole-life insurance

The main focus in high-cash-value, whole-life insurance is safe accumulation of cash and not the death benefit or the insured (the person whose life is insured). The insured could be you, your spouse, your child, your son-in-law, or your grandchildren. The owner of the policy maintains complete control of the cash and decisions about beneficiaries. The insured is simply the life the insurance is based on, but has no say in policy decisions.

Money can be taken out of the policy's cash value through withdrawals for loans. Withdrawals are not recommended because of possible taxes if you withdraw past your cost basis; you could lose the continued growth potential of the money that is taken out. A better option is through policy loans. There are no tax consequences if you borrow beyond your cost basis (what you've put in). Loans keep the policy cash value growing and working for you, it keeps the death benefit high, and it makes you accountable for the money you use. By borrowing money from the insurance company, you ensure that your capital never stops compounding.

You can close your policy at any time and get the cash or surrender value in the policy. You will be required to pay taxes on any policy growth above what you have contributed. When you close the policy, you may lose the possibility of further insurance ability depending on your health condition. You have also eliminated your financial legacy to your family and children. This is why we want to die with this policy intact. If you are unable to continue to pay the premiums, you do have an option inside the policy to eliminate future premiums or out-of-pocket payment, and simply let your cash value grow. This is referred to as a "reduced paid up" policy. This still gives you access to the cash value, which continues to grow while keeping the policy in force.

It is not recommended that you ever close the policy because you will lose the death benefit and be required to pay taxes on anything above what you have contributed (cost basis). The annual cash-value increase, total cash value, and death benefits in the current assumption column in the above charts are based on the dividends scale as of August 2019. Dividends can change and are not guaranteed; however, both Guardian and Mass Mutual insurance companies have paid dividends every year for more than 150 years. The specific numbers may vary, depending on the individual's age and health. To learn more about the infinite-banking concept, find the right agent, get examples of illustrations created for your specific individual needs, check out the resources at **PersonalBank4U.com or call (610) 681-2655.**

Strategy 5

Enjoy Life, Liberty, and the Pursuit of Happiness

Enjoying Good Health

ABOUT THREE YEARS AGO, I noticed that my computer IT guy had lost a considerable amount of weight. He was six-foot-two, and when I first met him, he weighed around 300 pounds. Within six months, he had dropped 100 pounds and now looked great. I was amazed because I disliked exercise and had always had trouble losing weight, so I asked him what his secret was.

He told me that weight loss was pretty much 90% diet and 10% exercise. He said he changed his eating habits and moved to a high-fat, low-carbohydrate, ketogenic method of eating. He recommended a site called Dietdoctor.com, which was founded in 2011 and has more than 55,000 members worldwide, making it the largest low-carb site in the world. It is filled with many articles, experts, videos, and low-carb recipes.

At that time, I was five-foot-six and weighed about 200 pounds, with a beautiful potbelly. Within three months of taking his advice, I lost more than 35 pounds and have maintained my weight at 165 pounds for the past three years. I walk a couple of miles once a week and do some weightlifting two times a week to keep my muscle tone. I take multivitamins, vitamin D, magnesium, and fish oil. I can now sleep eight hours a night, and I feel better than I have for years.

Another great website to help transform your health is http://drhyman.com/. Dr. Mark Hyman is an American physician and a *New York Times* bestselling author. He is the founder and medical director of the Ultra Wellness Center and director of the Cleveland Clinical Center for Functional Medicine.

Creating Great Relationships

Warren Buffett gives the following advice: *"Be around people that you admire and enjoy. They usually have an upbeat attitude about life, they're humorous, have integrity and are generous people who are thinking about what they can do for you. These qualities that you admire are not innate at birth, and you can acquire them. Then there are those negative qualities that turn you off in people who always need to be right and that you don't enjoy being with. You can choose what person you want to be, so why not choose the person you admire? Take your five best friends, mentors or your heroes, and write down the qualities that you like about them. Incorporate these qualities in your life, and eliminate the qualities of the people that turn you off. It's that simple. It is important to work with people in your life, and you will get the best out of people if they like you. You need to develop these habits now. Incorporate the great qualities now and eliminate the bad qualities, and you will have an incredible life. Choose your heroes very carefully because they will define you. You are one of your children's favorite heroes."*

Buffett also said that the secret to long-lasting relationships is low expectations. A friend told me that relationships improved immensely when you give up the need to be right. My wife, Nancy, and I were married in 1969. We have five children and thirteen grandchildren. We have had our ups and downs, but we are very supportive of each other. And if she has a problem that I know I can fix immediately, I listen intently and never offer advice. (There is a great and funny YouTube clip called *"It's Not About the Nail"* that makes this point very clear.)

Another great book is *The Five Love Languages,* by Gary Chapman. The five love languages are words of positive affirmation, acts of service, receiving gifts, quality time, and physical touch. Because I was abandoned as a child, my language is positive affirmation. This will fill up my love tank, while criticism will empty it. Even though I do some stupid things sometimes, Nancy is not critical of my errors. My wife's love language is quality time and acts of service. If she has something for me to do, such as change the burned-out light bulb in the kitchen, I immediately do it.

When I see my underwear drawer full, I know she did the laundry, and I thank her. I often tell her how beautiful she is and how much I love her. Even though our children may do things that we do not like, we provide advice only when asked, are never judgmental or critical, and are there to love them no matter what happens in their lives. Warren Buffett said he never met a truly successful person who did not have a great relationship with their children. Are you truly successful?

One last comment: I would never be in a relationship that is toxic or does not add true meaning to my life. Sadly, this toxicity could be from parents who are always judgmental and critical of you. Tell any toxic person that if they continue to be judgmental or critical, you will not be seeing them. I give you permission to take care of yourself first, or else you will not be good to anyone else. Think about what you are teaching your children about the type of relationship they should be in.

Creating Love in Your Life

Love is that special feeling we get when we have a connection with people and things in our life. It is created when we initiate and give love to people and things. Somebody could love us, and yet we may not feel anything. But we always feel love when we are loving others. We are fortunate to be in a profession where we can love our patients, our team, what we do, and, especially, our family. This doesn't apply only to loving people but also to things in our lives such as a good movie, a book, a special mug, and other things we go back to and create that feeling of love. Like the movie, *Love Actually* is all around us.

Learning and Understanding Meditation

Meditation helps reduce your stress, increase your energy, clear your brain, and relax the body for a deeper, more restful sleep. It makes you feel more connected, less anxious, and helps you to be calmer and more clear-headed in demanding situations. It can help you experience better relationships and sharpens your life focus. To learn a simple and powerful form of meditation, I recommend the new book written by Emily Fletcher entitled, *Stress Less, Accomplish More: Meditation for Extraordinary Performance.* For a better understanding of the Zeva Technique of meditation, check out her website: https://zivameditation.com/online/ or watch her YouTube video https://www.youtube.com/watch?v=yy6uOoMzbPg.

Letting Go of Issues and Emotional Pain from Your Past

When I was three years old, my mother divorced my father, and he moved to another city. My mother had to go back to school to get her degree, and my brothers and I lived with my grandmother for the next five years. At that young age, I subconsciously blamed myself for their divorce because if I could had been a better little boy this would not have happened. I carried this shame and pain through adulthood, hoping that no one would find out how bad I was. I subconsciously stuffed this emotional pain and started to feel from my brain—where there was no pain—not from my heart. This inability to feel deep emotions affected many in my personal and business relationships. I can easily understand why many men are not emotional. Once I addressed the issue and let go of this emotional pain, which can be easily done with proper techniques, my life and my self became more emotionally alive and peaceful. Many people carry deeply embedded emotional pain from their past that affects and controls their lives. This could be from abandonment (divorce), which I experienced, sexual abuse, not being wanted; there are many more. One group I worked with who are exceptionally good in helping individuals to identify, address, and let go of these issues is Legacy Life Consulting. Contact them at: https://www.legacylifeconsulting .com/ David Stamation (208) 946-3894.

You Need to Take Care of Yourself First

Many people feel they are serving others by giving away all their time and energies helping others, but, by doing so, they are not taking care of themselves, leaving them feeling exhausted, frustrated, and angry. This is especially true with women. The sad part is, they could better serve and help others if they took care of their own needs first. They need to set time aside just for themselves to love and nurture themselves first, and they will feel much better, less resentful, and happier as they serve others. The magic word that they need to use more often is "No, I can't do that. Thanks for asking."

Teaching Your Children About Finances

Mahatma Gandhi was asked what his message to the world was. He said, "My life is my message." Teach your children the satisfaction of being a saver instead of a spender. You need to show them the satisfaction of accomplishment and doing a job well done. Be the example for them of how they can find fun and joy in everything they do, instead of teaching them duty, responsibility, and that you must work hard for a living.

Teach your children to understand the ideas in this book. Help your children find a job, to learn to love work, save, and be disciplined with their money. Show them the power of getting out of debt and creating their own Personal Bank. Teach them the value of money and the feeling of freedom associated with being debt free.

Finding Happiness

When we get to be between 40 and 50 years old, our lives change. Many of us go through a clinical depression because we have lost the excitement of starting our careers or our business. Things may be going smoothly. The kids may be in college. But life changes, even if we don't want to admit it. We don't make changes in our work life anymore, and we don't care if it gets any better; we just hope it doesn't get any worse. Sometimes we take up hobbies instead of creating excitement in our work lives. As we reach midlife, it's time to realize that this is it; it's not going to get any better; it's all in our minds. We need to recognize this as an opportunity to go to work happy every day and to change our relationship to work so that it is fun. Life can be exciting if we let it be.

The future does not exist except in our imaginations; the past is merely a trace in our minds. The brain changes our recollections to fit our own convenience and purposes. This is also true with our work lives. Once we understand that we are working on a day-to-day basis, not a year-to-year basis, our attitudes and philosophies change, and, incidentally, we become more prosperous and have more fun.

I have consistently found that those who were happy while they were working are also happy during their retirement years. The opposite is also true: those who did not enjoy their work don't find any more happiness in retirement than they did while they were working.

The life and business coach Kendrick Mercer once had a fifty-year-old client from North Carolina. The client told him he had hated his work for the past twenty-five years. The worst problem was that he could not quit because he owed so much money. Kendrick told him he could set up his finances to be economically free in ten years, but he knew his client's problem was deeper than finances, so he asked him, "Once you reach financial freedom, what are you going to do?"

"I would first quit my practice," the client told him.

"Then what are you going to do?" Mercer asked.

"I am going to golf," he replied.

"Then what are you going to do?" Mercer asked.

He said, "I will buy a place on the beach and walk on the beach."

"Great," Mercer said. "Then what are you going to do?"

"Then I will watch TV and read books."

"Then what are you going to do?" Mercer asked him one more time.

He became sad and somber and said, "I will just walk on the beach some more."

"Great! What are you going to do then?"

He started to cry and said, "I'm going to die."

This is a pretty sad story. There was no real aliveness to this man, just a dead story. Mercer's fifty-year-old client was trying to get someplace instead of loving his life.

Mercer told him, "My job is to assist you in knowing that life is never going to be any better or worse than it is right now. It's just how you're looking at it. For you to go back and spend one more day losing your life for some future time which does not sound all that exciting will make your life a failure."

The client did not like hearing this, but he knew it was true. Mercer told him to go home and change his mind and outlook so he could enjoy dentistry again and appreciate his patients, his staff, and all his relationships. If he did this and still did not enjoy dentistry, then he should quit, sell everything, and do something with his life that he enjoyed.

The dentist did go back and created a new story for himself and his practice, and then he began to enjoy his practice. Kendrick coached him to slow down and sell some things to get rid of his debt. The client finally started to relax. Because life is lived in the present, it will truly never get any better or worse than it is this minute. It's all a matter of how we look at our experiences. This principle is the same for each one of us.

I have helped individuals become debt free and financially secure. Yet many tell me they are not happy. What I learned from Kendrick Mercer is that we carry many family imprints, negative emotional experiences such as abandonment or abuse, that make us feel that we are not worthy of happiness. We need to address these issues and let go of the loss and pain from the past. Sometimes, we need counseling to help us through this process.

One company that I have worked with which has helped me and my clients and their employees in identifying what holds them back from enjoying and finding peace in every aspect of their lives, resulting in more peace and happiness, is Legacy Life Consulting (http://legacylifeconsulting.com/).

It's Never Too Late

You may be in your 50s or even 60s and feel stuck in your business and in your life. Just like the story above, you can reassess your business and life, and make changes now. I've worked with many clients in their 50s and 60s, helping them through the process of making their business more efficient and fun while working fewer days. We also talked about getting rid of the junk in your life. Junk is defined as anything that does not add meaning to your life.

First, find out what your net worth is by writing down all your assets and debts. Look at your business, and eliminate everything that does not make it fun. This may include employees who are negative and cause drama. Once you become much more profitable, you could decide to sell your business and move to a different part of the country, where it may be warmer or where you can be closer to your children and work part time. When you clear your mind and are open to all possibilities, the choices become endless.

As you go through this process, make sure you have your spouse on board. The junk you want to eliminate may include the large boat you use only two to three weeks out of the year but costs you $1000 in slip fees and maintenance each month. You may have had a loss in an individual investment such as a stock or limited partnership. Realize that you already have taken the loss and that chances are great that it will never come back. However, your keeping this loss distracts you from moving on and learning from your lesson. So just sell it, and use the loss to offset your gains in other investments. The only exception are stocks that drop during a down market, because you should never sell in a down market. You may have rental property that causes you a lot of headaches and produces low financial returns. It may be the large house with high maintenance costs which you could sell and move into a new or smaller home or condo and invest the difference in your retirement account. Go through your closet, and get rid of all clothes and shoes that you have not worn in the past year. Getting rid of junk in your life gives you great peace of mind and contentment. Now you can focus on creating strong relationships with your spouse and your children.

How Much Do You Need in Retirement?

Many financial advisers tell you that you need 70% of your current income to be comfortable in retirement. I think one reason they say this is to make sure you keep investing more money in their actively managed funds. You will probably need only between 25% and 35% of your current income. Let me summarize and do the math: Take your current income—let's say $120,000.

When you are retired, you will not need to pay taxes on your working income or put away for retirement, so you can subtract out 20% for taxes and 20% for retirement; and you're down to $72,000. Subtract out 5% for insurance, 5% for child-related costs, and 15% for your mortgage. You're now down to $42,000. Subtract out another 1% for job-related expenses, 2% for reduced charitable contributions, and 1% for reduced housing expenses. You're down to $37,200. Add back in, say, 10% for increased travel costs and 5% for increased healthcare costs. This moves us up to $55,200. Subtract out $36,000 for Social Security, and that leaves us at $19,200, or 16% of our current income.

The Illusion That Money Will Make Us Happy

Most Americans fall prey to the illusion that money will make us happy. There are more miserable, depressed, and anxious millionaires than you can imagine! I've seen clearly and repeatedly that money will *not* buy happiness. Nothing that money can buy will make you happy on an ongoing basis, and many people resent those who have money. This attitude will prevent them from creating abundance in their lives.

The belief that money will make us happy seems almost unstoppable. It is one of the big illusions that keeps us from developing integrity with money. Some people think that, if they win the lottery, they will be happy, but things never seem to work out that way. Money can make people miserable because of their false expectation of what it will bring. What makes us happy is having integrity in every aspect of our lives, including expressing our feelings through travel, love, and relationships.

On some level, we all know money will not make us happy, but we still act *as if* it will. Money does bring a certain kind of security that we wouldn't otherwise have. With that security, perhaps we can express happiness or enjoy life more consistently. Being financially secure is different from being rich. *Happiness comes from enjoying each moment and appreciating everything that comes into our lives. It comes from helping others. This is where the real fun is. As we give love to others, we can't stop the abundance of love that comes into our own lives.*

No precise dollar amount translates into this capacity. On the other hand, poor money management (such as having high debt and many creditors) can make you unhappy, and that is one good reason for developing a clear financial context. Sometimes it takes buying the things you always thought you wanted before you realize that they alone do not bring you happiness. Spending without a clear guide diffuses and wastes your money and your financial freedom. If you have a clear context about money, you'll *rent* the boat or vacation home you've dreamed of first, to see if it really does add meaning to your life.

Jonathan Clements, in his must-read book *The Little Book of Main Street Money: 21 Simple Truths That Help Real People Make Real Money,* says that buying things might bring us happiness but not long-lasting happiness. Over the past decades, we, as a society, have made vast improvements in our standard of living, yet people still aren't any happier. We need to get off the treadmill and think about how we spend our money and how we spend our time. Clements makes six recommendations for happiness.

- Buy experiences rather than things.
- Count your blessings.
- Strive for a sense of control.

- Find a purpose instead of trying to create endless leisure time.
- Give a little, volunteer, or donate.
- Make time for friends and family.

There is a wealth of information on his website, which is always updated and worth visiting. https://humbledollar.com/money-guide/main-menu/

Stop Complaining

Half of the people think you deserve what you get, and the other half don't care. Kendrick Mercer shared a story with me after his three-month sailing from California to Lahaina, Maui. His trip was an incredible adventure, with beautiful sunny days, stormy weather, moonbows at night and wonderful solitude. After arriving in Lahaina, he took a plane to Honolulu. He was enjoying the view over the ocean while a lady sitting next to him was complaining to him about her life, children, and husband. During the break in her conversation, he looked at her and said, "Let's play a game. Let's pretend the plane breaks right in half, and we are all going to die. All you see in front of you is blue sky. We have two choices: we can grab on to the armrest in terror and think about all the things we didn't do in our life, or we can calmly unbuckle our seatbelts, stand up, jump forward, and fly for the rest of our lives." She did not say much after that but gave him a big hug at the end of the flight. Why not live our life in gratitude and enjoy every moment?

Cultural and Family Imprinting

I realized that, before my clients could be at peace with money, they had to open and address the deeper behavioral issues keeping them from having integrity with money and with life. Our attitudes toward money can keep us from living full and peaceful lives. We have all inherited a range of imprints from our families of origin concerning money. These imprints often include prejudices, insecurities, and false assumptions, which pull us away from developing integrity with money. We tend to repeat the clichés about money that we learned as children, even if they're not true, such as "You can never have enough money," "It takes money to make money," "The poor working man can never get ahead" and "You must work hard for your money."

Most people who have plenty of money keep working, not because they enjoy it or choose to, but because working has come to represent worthiness. It is a kind of cultural fad. Work seems to justify our very right to exist. Your family imprint for duty, responsibility, and working hard for a living may be incredibly strong, or perhaps work has become an addiction. Many people work because that is what society expects them to do, or because their parents told them they'd be bums if they didn't work hard six days a week. Our current attitudes about money tend to limit our choices, even when we have achieved wealth. The ideal balance would be to have a great deal of money and at the same time to be at peace, doing only what we really want to do. For most of us, our lives are half over, and it is time to have some fun now! You cannot create what you cannot envision. Get very clear about making your life fun and enjoyable: feel it, and keep moving toward that vision. Bring your vision to your office and your family. Don't settle for anything less. Take time to talk to your children, not about duty or responsibility, but about what brings happiness, fun, and joy into their lives and what it will take to create that story for them.

How Do We Define Success?

This can be different for each one of us. For me, it is about loving what I do each day, being at peace in my life, being in good health, having time to be with and enjoy the people I love, being debt free, having enough money that I don't worry about money anymore, and having the time and resources to make a difference in the world around me. Others may define success as being the best businessman, making a lot of money, having time to do missionary work, retiring at age 55, having $2 million in the bank—the list goes on. This book is not meant to define your success but to show you how to have enough time and money to make choices in your life that are right for you. *It's not about making a living. It's about making a life worth living.*

French writer François-René de Chateaubriand (1768 to 1848) said, *"A master in the art of living draws no sharp distinction between his work and his play; his labor and his leisure; his mind and his body; his education and his recreation. He hardly knows which is which; he simply pursues his vision of excellence through whatever he is doing, and leaves others to determine whether he is working or playing. To himself, he always appears to be doing both."*

How Much Is Enough?

If you are like most people in the world, one bowl of rice a day would be enough. Here in America, we think in terms of economic freedom. In my past book *Time and Money,* I define economic freedom as the day you have accumulated enough safe, liquid assets that can reproduce your lifestyle income (the amount of money it takes to maintain your lifestyle), with safeguards against inflation, for the rest of your life, without touching the principal. This will vary by individual, but once you are debt free, you could reach that point in five to seven years, simply by following the recommendations in this book.

THE NEW RETIREMENT PARADIGM

Make a Difference in the World

There is a difference between success and significance. One of the great advantages of having more time and more money is the ability to make a difference in the lives of people in the world around us. One reason I enjoy going into the office two days a week is that I can create abundance to share with others. Because I am debt free, each year, I significantly donate to many great causes, including the Union Gospel Mission dental clinic for our street people, Safe Place for battered women, the food banks, a dental assisting program, my church and various other causes that make a difference in the world around me. I believe that this brings even more abundance into my life. Even though you are working on paying off debt, donate either your time or money to an important cause. This will make a difference in your life and those you help.

The Two-Dollar-Bill Story of Finding Happiness

I love giving out two-dollar bills as a reminder of our freedom in the United States. This $2 bill is the only piece of US currency that depicts the same person on the front and standing on the back. On the front of the bill, we see Thomas Jefferson, the third president of the United States. Then we turn the bill over and see him signing the Declaration of Independence. The people standing around the table are the committee who wrote the declaration. The main author is Thomas Jefferson (the tall person in the center). The person standing on the far left is John Adams, the second president of the United States.

John Adams and Thomas Jefferson had a few things in common: They were both presidents and were the only presidents who signed the Declaration of Independence. They both died on

July 4, within three hours of each other, exactly fifty years after they signed the Declaration of Independence.

In those days, the average man lived to age thirty-five. Adams was ninety, and Jefferson was eighty-three on the day they died. I believe the reason they lived two to three generations beyond the average man is that they were both highly motivated to instill and imprint the ideals of freedom and independence into our American culture. They lived with a purpose.

This is what makes the United States one of the freest countries in the world; we can work and live anywhere we want in this country. We are free to be in any mutual relationship we want and to leave it if it is toxic (a relationship where you will never grow and are always being put down).

Sadly, most Americans don't know they are free. Many feel trapped in their lives, business, jobs, and relationships. They feel angry, controlled, frustrated, anxious, or sad. These feelings come from a place of fear—many people fear change and have one foot in and one foot out of their choices (relationships or jobs). These feelings immediately disappear when the person acts, after choosing to change, or by putting "both feet in or out" of their choice.

The $2 bill reminds us of our choice to be free, independent, and happy. The secret of happiness is in three choices. Any time you feel upset, angry, or trapped, there is something in your life that you are not accepting. The courage to make one of these three choices will give you back your freedom and peace of mind. The choices are as follows:

1. You can change your situation (relationship or work), which takes courage as you face and conquer your fears. For example, if someone is always judgmental or critical of you and this is a deal-breaker, then you can tell them that behavior is no longer acceptable to you and that, if they continue, you will leave the relationship. If they stop this unacceptable behavior, then you will stay and be at peace. If not, you choose number two.

2. You can leave the situation (e.g., relationship or work).

3. If you can't change the situation or you choose not to leave the situation, then you can stay and accept the "what is" of the situation and be totally at peace with the situation because it is your choice. We need to change "Why is this happening to me?" **to** "Why is this happening **for** me?"

Summary

-   First, write your new money story, and set your goals for increasing your income, eliminating your debt first and then increasing your savings in your Personal Bank.

-   Create a business you love—one that is profitable—and then do more of it. Learn to make more money and focus that money toward debt reduction. Once you are debt free, you should consider creating a Personal Bank. For more information go to personalbank4U. com. Many business owners I coach complain about some of the people they work with who make them miserable. I tell them to go back to their office and tell the owner to fire those people. Then I remind them that *they are the owner.* Most people forget that they can make their business exactly what they want it to be. They have the canvas and the brush.

- Stop listening to the news and worrying about what's happening in the market or the country. This is just noise. That's it. Now, enjoy your life, be grateful, and spend the rest of your money on things that add meaning to your life. This leads to financial freedom and a life of self-integrity and peace.

- Economic peace of mind is more than just financial freedom. In fact, we can experience economic peace of mind long before we reach financial freedom. *Once we have a solid guide in place for achieving financial freedom, we can let go of our anxiety about money and live as if it has already happened.* With this newfound peace of mind, we can truly enjoy life in the moment because we are secure in what we have, and we know that we can deal with any life challenge.

Now we can face life with joy and excitement once we have a vision and a beautiful story for our lives. With this book, each of us can claim both financial freedom *and* economic and personal peace of mind. "Being happy is a choice."

About the Author

DR. ALBERT "ACE" GOERIG graduated from Case Western Reserve University Dental School in 1971 and was their distinguished alumnus in 2014. Following graduation, he joined the US Army and retired as a colonel in 1991. In 1996 he began coaching doctors and their teams how to create personal and financial freedom in their lives. His most recent book, *Dr. Ace's Guide to Personal and Financial Freedom,* was published in 2019 and was an Amazon international best seller. He has a free website, DoctorAce.com, with audios and videos to help individuals quickly become debt free and eventually financially free. He and his wife, Nancy, were married in 1969. They have five children and 13 grandchildren.

www.ingramcontent.com/pod-product-compliance
Lightning Source LLC
Chambersburg PA
CBHW031900200326
41597CB00012B/492